ON EA

David Adam was b
berland, and is nov
He was Vicar of 1
for over 20 years, ~
for composing prayers in the Celtic pattern.
His first book of these, *The Edge of Glory*,
achieved immediate popularity. His books
have been translated into various languages,
including Finnish and German, and have
appeared as American editions. Much of the
present book arises from talks, lectures and
events on Holy Island, and from pilgrimage
to other holy places.

ON EAGLES' WINGS

The Life and Spirit of St Chad

DAVID ADAM

Illustrated by
Nikki Bovis-Coulter

TRIANGLE

First published in Great Britain in 1999
Triangle
Society for Promoting Christian Knowledge
Holy Trinity Church
Marylebone Road
London NW1 4DU

British Library Cataloguing-in-Publication Data

A catalogue record for this book is available from
the British Library

ISBN 0-281-05216-6

Typeset in Garamond Light by
Pioneer Associates, Perthshire
Printed in Great Britain by
Caledonian International Ltd, Glasgow

Contents

Introduction

I have been privileged to live and learn at Lindisfarne for nine years. Much of the island has still the same feel as in the days of Aidan and his first students. The seals still sing and the tide still ebbs and flows, Orion still rises and promises storms. Within the parish church of St Mary the Virgin, we maintain a rhythm of daily prayer, though now it is a mere three services every day. Each day, three times a day, the bell rings out and calls people to worship near where Chad and his brothers worshipped. Pilgrims come from all over the world to this small village and island because of the saints who have lived here. Saints from here travelled the length and breadth of England and on to the continent of Europe with the Good News of Christ. It is also interesting to see the strong links there were with Ireland.

I have also had the privilege of living on the North Yorkshire moors, 'the place of wild beasts and of people who live like wild beasts'. I have walked across 'Blackamoor' many times on a pilgrimage to Lastingham. In my last parish there was the 'little shieling of Colman'; it is said he stayed there on his visit to Whitby. Whilst living at Danby I had the honour of being a canon of York Minister, where for a short time Chad was bishop. So I feel that I have many links with Chad and his brothers. I note that Bede calls these four lads

'Northumbrians' rather than English. I like that, for it is what I am myself. In the very make-up of so many who are now called English there are the people who were there before the arrival of these 'invaders' – the British, or as some would call them, the Celts. Some of us still feel more British than English. Maybe it is for this reason that we find an attraction in some of these early saints.

It was my good fortune to have been brought up with stories of the Northumbrian saints. Aidan, Cedd, Chad, Cuthbert were local folk heroes. Their stories were told in school and there was a feeling that these men were still living just up the road on Lindisfarne. The stories were told as if these holy men were actually still at work and doing all those wonderful and heroic acts. My father was a Scot and a romantic. He loved to point out Lindisfarne as we passed by on the Great North Road. 'That's the place of the saints,' he would say. I was under the impression that they were there and still at work. I still have this impression as I now work on Lindisfarne. The saints do not seem very far away in time or space. It is wonderful to share in the Communion of Saints.

Without the work of Aidan, Cedd, Chad and the Celtic monasteries, the work of dividing up England into parishes by Archbishop Theodore would not have been possible. Many places were ministered to by Celtic-trained priests. The Celtic monasteries provided 'minsters' from which priests went out in mission and then returned for fellowship and support. These early parish priests knew how to work as teams, and in team ministry. People like Chad and his brothers helped to set the Church in this land on a firm foundation. It is good to look at their lives and what inspired them, so that we too may be inspired. We can still learn from their seeking to make God the priority of their lives. We can be enriched by their earthiness and their deep love for the world as well as for its creator. My hope is that looking at such inspiring people will help us to soar on eagles' wings, and to put our trust and hope in our God.

At the end of each chapter I have put some simple exercises. There is a psalm to read; far better if you learn it. Remember, the students in the early monasteries learnt all the Psalms off by heart. The Psalms are a wonderful resource when our own words and prayers fail us. I still say the Psalter through once a month, but I remember that some of the Celtic saints, like Egbert, said the whole of the Psalter from memory every day. It was not just a learning of words but a relationship with the God to whom the words were addressed. I have used here the Psalms from *Celebrating Common Prayer* (published by Mowbray). The second exercise is usually to make you stretch your mind and think about what has gone before. Finally there is a prayer to end each chapter. For any Bible readings I have used the New International Version.

Like all my books, this one began in talking to people about the Celtic saints of this land, listening to what pilgrims and visitors had to tell me, and from my giving a lecture or taking a retreat on the Celtic saints and what they can teach us.

I would like to thank Daibhi O Croinin for his research on Rathmelsigi and showing that the most likely place for it is in County Carlow.

1

The Journey to Lindisfarne

Travelling over the sands was very exciting for the four brothers, for they seemed to be going out to sea. Their horses were splashing in the watery sands beneath them: this was a marvellous place for anyone wanting to ride at speed. It took them all their self-restraint not to race against each other. Never had the brothers faced such a wide expanse. They were more used to openings in the forests; this was like entering a new world. To the left of them were sand dunes covered in grasses but no signs of life apart from birds. It all seemed very wild and lacking in trees. Away far to the right, over endless sands, towered the fortress of Bamburgh where Oswald was the king. The brothers could see silver smoke rising from the area. It was Oswald who was responsible for them being here today, if not directly then indirectly, for he had invited the monk Aidan to come from Iona to teach the Angles. Oswald believed that Christianity would be the uniting factor between the ancient people of the land and his own incoming Angles.

The father of the four boys rode out in front, determined to be the leader and guiding them to the small rising land on the horizon. It was not possible to ride to the south because of the river that curled over the sands as it went out to sea. Ceawlin had been warned that this was not a safe place, there are quicksands, and sometimes the tide

5

rushes in and catches the unwary: many lives had been lost in crossing to and from Lindisfarne. He had been assured that it was safe to cross the tidal stretch this afternoon as long as he was off again before the tide was two hours to its peak; later than that and his horse would be swimming. Because it was a time of a half moon the tides were not so deep, and that is why the monks had invited him to come over the sands on this day. Ceawlin trusted these men he was visiting for their sending him the message about the tide. A greater trust, however, was being asked of him, in that he had been asked to leave his four sons with the monks of Lindisfarne.

How Ceawlin heard of Aidan and his monks we do not know. It is possible that he was a person of some importance and had contact with King Oswald. Perhaps Oswald had suggested that his boys would be ideal for the school on the island. The older ones Ceawlin could well imagine being trained and sent out; but what of Chad, his youngest? The lad was but a child, even though he was growing up quickly. Today he could see Chad enjoying the adventure, but when left with these strange monks, away from home, he might quickly change his tune.

With the five horsemen were a few men from Ceawlin's estate bringing gifts and food for the monks and some planking for houses. Ceawlin let the cart set the pace for their travelling; it was important that they all kept together. He had been told that the education of the boys would be free. There was no charge, though in turn each of the boys would be expected to provide for the others; if they did not have any funds they would do it through labour or through begging for food.

Ceawlin certainly did not like the idea of his boys begging like the countless poor who were around, he must see if he could provide for them in some way. He would pay the fosterage tithe that was normal for any child sent to live with another family, that is if these monks actually dealt with money. If not, they might like grain, honey and wood until they had set their own farms up and running.

As they rode on the curlew cried overhead, a sad song, a song of the moors as well as the sea. Their crying made Chad think of home and their farm. He would miss his mother and the rest of the family. He would miss the friends of his own age with whom he had mock battles. He had thought of becoming a warrior when he grew up, and fighting for the king; now he was going to be a soldier of the great King, or so his father had told him. Already Chad had heard that these holy men were called soldiers of Christ. He had heard that they fought battles against demons and powers of darkness; they even challenged the devil himself. Thinking of these terrors, Chad began to wonder whether he ought to return home with his father. But that would be to act like a baby and a coward. He was growing to be a strong young man and he must show that he was not afraid. Anyhow if Cedd, Caelin and Cynebil could become warriors for Christ, so could he.

This little group poses us a few unanswered questions. Where did they come from? Where did their Christian faith come from, if the monks of Lindisfarne were the first to bring Christianity to Northumbria? Bede tells us the boys were North-umbrians, so we know they belonged to the area somewhere between the Forth and the Humber; it is likely that they were from not too far from Lindisfarne or Bamburgh. Were they Angles or were they British? Or to ask it another way, were they English or Celtic? This we shall never know. Could it be that they were both, and so ideally suited for the Lindisfarne mission? The year was 635 so it was almost a hundred years since Ida the Flamebearer had invaded the land of the British, and built his stockade at Bamburgh. The last great battle of the British was here on the edge of the sands they were crossing. In this very area, Urien ap Rheged, a Christian king, died trying to drive the pagan Angles into the sea. Even that was now history for it was over fifty years ago. The battle that Urien lost reminds us that this area between the Forth and the Humber was a Christian country. It may be that Christianity was not a majority religion, but it was well established, at least in some areas. At the Roman Wall area there has recently been found a Christian church from the fifth century. It is also thought that St Patrick came from the western end of the wall. Patrick's father was a deacon and his grandfather a priest, so Christianity was not new to the region. But until now, the British had not attempted to convert the English, which is not surprising when the English came as the conquerors. By the seventh century there was a growing together of the peoples; there was intermarriage between the Angles who were now settled and the local indigenous British. More often now it was not the conquering of a people that was bringing together the different factions but the joining of families in marriage. It could just be that these lads were of such a mixed marriage. If that were the case they would be ideally suited for the task ahead of uniting the two groups into one nation. It would also mean that they were already bi-lingual and could speak a Celtic language as well as that of the Angles. If you look at the names of this family they do look like an Anglicized form of Celtic names: the four boys were called Cedd, Cynebil, Caelin and Ceadda; the last of these names is usually shortened to Chad. Because we are always given the names in this order we assume that Cedd was the oldest and Chad the youngest. It is likely that all of the boys were teenagers and that this was a great adventure for them, though Celtic monasteries did take in children for training as young as seven.

Glancing back to see that his boys were all following, Ceawlin could see the Cheviot mountain rearing its massive head over the nearby hills. In the mellowness of the day it looked as if it were blue and not 'white topped' as its name means in the Celtic language. They were now coming to the island proper, the wet sand was giving way to sandy fields and scrub. To the south they could see the smoke rising from a fire but they could see no sign of houses. Looking around it seemed promising land, it should be good for growing crops if they could stand the salt spray from the sea. There were clumps of hazel and willow, but most of the bushes leaned at an angle which showed there was a predominance of very strong westerly winds. Ceawlin could see to the south-east in the distance an outcrop of rock; perhaps the village would be there, for it could have a fortress on the top. However, the smoke was coming from the south end of the island so they followed the smoke. Now, after a quarter of a mile, Ceawlin could see huts in a small enclosure; they were obviously new and some were not yet finished. He wondered to what sort of place and people he had brought his lads. Could anything come of this little settlement? There was nothing that looked noble or comfortable, nor did it look as if it could be easily defended. These men were having to build a village for themselves before they could do anything else. The farming of the land had not yet started. The most striking object within the enclosure was a large wooden standing cross, which was about the height of two men.

The group of riders had been seen, and now someone was coming to meet them. As he came he wiped his hands on the rough apron he was wearing as a protection for his other clothes. This was not a big man but he was obviously a confident man. He greeted them, but Ceawlin was not sure of the words. Aidan, though soft-spoken, was a man of great might. As Aidan did not know much of the Anglian language it was necessary to keep the words few and simple: even Aidan's Celtic tongue was not quite like the language of the British in Northumbria; Ceawlin would learn that that was because Aidan was originally from Ireland. But though his tongue was different from the Celtic-speaking British, there were enough words in common for the two men to communicate. Again Ceawlin glanced at the houses. His lads had been used to good housing; he really wondered where they would be put up and if there was room for the four of them. There were not as many as a dozen huts on the whole site, though a few more were nearly completed.

Aidan was obviously excited by the presence of the young men. These were to be among his first students; they were to be among the next generation of priests and maybe more – but that is dreaming and jumping too far ahead. Aidan felt that he was luckier than the priest Eli in the Bible, for here he was given four young men. He prayed to God that they might hear His voice and serve Him faithfully with Aidan in this land. At first, though their father had dismounted, the boys remained on their horses and Aidan had to look up to them to greet them. He called others across and they came welcoming and smiling at the boys; all of them had to look up to these young men on horseback. Aidan would remind Chad in particular of this in the years to come. Ceawlin saw the awkwardness of the situation and ordered his boys to dismount to be on the same level as the men who were attempting to speak to them. The lads were slow at getting down and were a little afraid of coming to greet the monks. 'These are my sons, Cedd, Cynebil, Caelin and Ceadda.' Chad was amazed at the firmness of the grasp of these monks; they did look like warriors even though there was no sign of any weapons. It was their strange hair-style that gave them the appearance of Celtic warriors. Each of them had shaved their hair from the front of their heads so that there was no hair in front of the ears; the whole forehead and half the top was bald. Chad found this quite fascinating and could hardly stop staring. The strangeness was accentuated by the fact that their hair grew long down the back. Chad suddenly wondered if his hair would be shaved like this and he began to fear. He looked at Aidan and caught a twinkle in

11

his eye and forgot his worry. Aidan looked a kindly, yet a tough man.

'*Dominus vobiscum.* Welcome in the name of the Lord. Ceawlin, we greet you and your family in the name of Christ our Saviour. They certainly all look like strong lads. You do not know how important they are to me. The unity of this country, the bonding together of various peoples will depend on such as these. Through our mission here the English and the British could become one people, serving one God. If they do their work properly they will join together that which was once at war and bring a deeper peace to our land. More than that, they are called to be the soldiers of the great King and will be asked to give their lives in His service.'

Ceawlin was not sure of all that Aidan said but he thought this was maybe not a bad place after all for the fosterage of his sons. Here, away from the mainland, they would be less likely to be raided. They would learn more than farming. They would learn to read and calculate. They would be able to speak from shapes on pieces of vellum and tell others what was written there. Here they would certainly learn discipline and how to become leaders of men. Ceawlin suddenly became anxious. If he stayed too long, perhaps Chad at least would want to come back home with him. He made the tide his excuse and said he needed to be away. Aidan, knowing there was plenty of time for the tide had hardly turned, tried to dissuade him and offered him a meal. Ceawlin pointed to Chad in a way that only Aidan noticed and shook his head. Aidan then understood and nodded to Ceawlin. It was now time to present the monks with gifts of vegetables, grain, honey, candles and wax, with the planking and the cart on which the planking was carried. Aidan thanked Ceawlin and then said, 'We will not need all these horses, we have not enough land to keep them on and we do not intend to be going far for a while. The few horses that we have on the island will do.' Ceawlin shuddered at this; he thought at least one of his boys would object. They were very attached to their horses, usually it was hard to get them to be separated from them. Horses were a symbol of authority and of wealth, of power and manhood. But the firmness in Aidan's voice convinced him to see to the removal of the horses. Immediately he got four of his workmen to take the reins from each boy and then he bid them all farewell. Chad nearly refused to let go until he caught a glance both of his father and of Aidan. There were tears in his eyes as all that was familiar to him seemed to move away. But at least he had his brothers and he was sure Cedd would look after him.

'Come and see what we have done,' said Aidan as he led the boys over the vallum and towards the huts. 'We have prepared this land with forty days of fasting and prayer. We set it aside to the glory of God, we cleansed it from evil, fighting against all demons and so reclaimed it for God and His goodness. This wall may not keep out an army, but it keeps the powers of evil at bay.' The boys were not sure that they understood all that Aidan was saying. His accent was very different from the dialect of the British that they knew. They looked at each other and secretly pulled faces to express puzzlement. Aidan continued, 'Here inside this circle will be your home. I will introduce you to the brothers you will live with.' Chad began to be afraid for he suddenly realized that he was to be separated from his brothers; each was being sent to a different hut. 'Come and meet your cell-mate, for he will be responsible for teaching you many things; in turn you will help him to understand the language of the English.' None of the brethren were very elderly, in fact all were strong young men. Chad looked upon his new lodgings with some disgust. The room was almost without furnishing, not much better than what was provided for cattle at home. The sleeping area was little more than a pile of straw and a covering of some sort. Yet its single occupant was friendly enough. Though the window was not glazed it had a shutter to keep out the wind. From the window it was possible to look back to the mainland and the high hills. 'Chad, I am to be your *anamchara,* your cell-mate, or as we say your soul friend. I have the responsibility for teaching you the faith and you will teach me to speak as the Angles do. We will begin tomorrow. Today let me show you around the island.' As they left the hut Chad could see Cedd already stepping out with his own soul friend. It was a pity he did not know what the words meant. To be called a cell-mate made him sound like a prisoner; perhaps that was what he now was. In a strange way he had been taken captive by these men and held on this little island. Maybe he would never escape from this new kind of captivity.

The sun was shining and the island was beautiful. Chad began to think it might not be so bad after all. They climbed the highest rock and looked all around them. Below to the west was another small island and beyond that the mainland; to the east was the wide sea dotted with a few more little islands. Down to the south was the capital, Bamburgh, where the king lived. Chad hoped they would be able to go there quite often. Northwards in the far distance were great cliffs, and inland high hills. Looking right around, Chad realized that his eyes could only take in a little at a time. This was a wide panorama indeed. 'We have called this the Heugh,' said his companion, 'and look, there are a couple of seals swimming in the sea below us.' Chad was delighted to see these great creatures and hardly noticed as his companion continued, 'Below the Heugh on the landward side are our houses; the hill protects them from some of the winds. Beyond the monastery we intend to grow our corn.' They walked further down the Heugh and met the rest of Chad's brothers. 'Here in the harbour we have a couple of boats beached, one is used for fishing and the other in our journeying to Bamburgh and beyond. Have you ever been out fishing?' Chad had to admit he had only fished in a river, never in the sea, but he would like to learn. 'I will teach you how to make nets and we will fish together. Listen! The bell is being struck; in a few moments it will be time for prayer. Come, let us go to the church.'

Chad had noticed the large oak building with the high wooden cross outside. Now his three brothers and the monks who were with them clambered down from the hillside. When they got to the church, each was shown where to stand; everyone faced the altar. Candles were lit and the lovely smell of honey mingled with the rich smell of wood. The oak planking of which the church was made had only recently been cut and adzed. The church had a mixture of smells, and Chad concentrated on these: wood and soil, candles and people, and there was just the faint smell of the sea. The brother next to him smelt of sheep and this made Chad feel more at home. In the silence, Chad could hear his own breathing as regular as the sound of the sea. For what appeared to be a long time everyone stood in silence, not a single word was spoken. Cedd gave a little wave across to Chad, hoping he would not be noticed by the monks. Chad waved back and Aidan smiled at them both.

When the service did begin, each of the boys could only listen. It was not in English, or in a British tongue, it was in Latin. Fortunately they were at least used to a Latin mass, so words here and there and an occasional sentence were familiar. They could reply to '*Dominus vobiscum*', they knew the Lord's Prayer and the Gloria and they knew the Kyries. The words ebbed and flowed like the sea; it sounded like poetry they were reciting, the sound of their voices echoing the sound of wind and waves outside. It was all very soothing and Chad began to feel quite sleepy, that is until he felt hungry and he began to wonder when they would eat. Suddenly the service ended. Again there was a long silence before anyone moved, then they all seemed to get up and go out at once. It was time to eat.

The refectory was much like the church, a single room made of oak planking. The tables and benches were of the same planking, though the adzing made them very smooth. There was a smell of newly-cut wood but no smell of food. Chad fancied a nicely cooked bird. He got this, but in its earliest stage; he was given an egg, a few green vegetables, and a chunk of bread, 'Eat up and enjoy it,' whispered his soul friend, 'for there will be no food tomorrow until three in the afternoon. Though if you feel weakly tomorrow, you can have some water. We will also keep silent from now on; there will be no speaking unless it is necessary, or to do with worship or work.' Chad no longer felt like eating, yet he ate it all, wondering how he would survive tomorrow until three in the afternoon. The idea of not talking also worried him. How would he spend his time without talking to the person he was with? He would willingly have left for home, but the tide was now in and his horse had been taken away.

Silence was to become part of the rhythm of Chad's life, and it began with this meal – though in fact, while everyone ate, one person was reading from a lectern. Chad did not understand a word, but it filled the silence. There were times over the next weeks, when if it were not for the sea or the wind, he might have thought he had gone deaf. He was slowly to discover that silence is a great teacher. In time, it became a pleasure to feel the silence after the calling of the bell or after the blessing at the end of a service. Silence became a time of not wanting to possess or to impress; it was a time to be possessed, to rest in God who is to be found in each of us and all about us. But this is racing ahead. At this moment the silence seemed to envelop Chad and its power was a little frightening.

He was soon in the cell with his new companion, the shutter had been closed on the window as had the door. Between their beds a little light flickered in a mussel shell. Chad watched the shadows dancing on the wall until the light burnt itself out. Apart from hearing the breathing of his companion and a strange moaning sound from outside, he felt very much alone. He would have sought out his brothers, but he did not dare. He could have wept but would not allow himself. When sleep came it was fitful and demon-visited. The moaning outside disturbed him, but he was not allowed to speak to his companion. In the dark it sounded as though demons or sea monsters were wanting to speak to him, and he was afraid. The sea itself roared like a great monster as Chad tossed and turned. He recited a prayer he had learnt to protect him from evil. Already he felt he was being called to spiritual warfare.

God is my helper
God is my guide
God is at my side
God is my protector
God is my shield
God is my strength.
I need not fear
For God is here.

The next day he was rather embarrassed to hear that the demons of the night were seals singing on the sandbanks at low tide. The song of the seals would be a sound he would forever associate with Lindisfarne and a sound he learnt to love.

EXERCISES

There were then four brothers, whom we have mentioned, Cedd, Cynebil, Caelin and Chad, who were all famous priests of the Lord, a very rare thing to happen, and two of them reached the rank of bishop (Bede, Book 3, Chapter 23, 1992).

1 Read, and if you can, learn Psalm 63
verses 1–8.

O God, you are my God; eagerly I seek you;
my soul thirsts for you, my flesh faints for you,
as in a barren and dry land where there is no
    water;

Therefore I have gazed upon you in your holy
    place,
that I might behold your power and your glory.

For your loving-kindness is better than life itself;
my lips shall give you praise.

So will I bless you as long as I live
and lift up my hands in your name.

My soul is content, as with marrow and fatness,
and my mouth praises you with joyful lips,

When I remember you upon my bed,
and meditate upon you in the night watches.

For you have been my helper,
and under the shadow of your wings I will rejoice.

My soul clings to you;
your right hand holds me fast.

PAUSE Keep silent and wait upon God. Learn that God speaks to those who can keep silent.

PICTURE The child Samuel was left by his mother with the old priest Eli. This was a gift the old man could have done without. Yet each day he would seek to teach Samuel. Every day Samuel would be attentive to and wait upon Eli. Samuel would gain wisdom from the heart of the old man. Each night the lad would listen in case the old man called for him. In this way his ears were being trained. There was much silence. Eli was losing his sight. Vision was failing. The Lamp of the Presence in the sanctuary was burning low and likely to go out. Into the situation came the voice of God. Three times Samuel heard the voice. Three times he went and disturbed the old man. Each time the old man tried to get the lad to go back and sleep. Then the nearly blind man saw, it was God himself calling this young lad. 'It is the Lord. It is God calling you. If it happens again say, "Speak, Lord, your servant is listening."' So Samuel was brought to understand and become aware of the presence and the voice of God.

PONDER Think on this story. See how it relates to the Church of today. Often the Church is thought of as old, lacking vision and letting the light go out. Often the young are asked not to disturb it, and let it sleep. But without the tradition handed down, without the wisdom of the old, the young will have no one to guide them and lead them to God. The young disturb the settled and encourage new vision and new hope, but they need the old to help them interpret life and its mysteries.

PROMISE To spend some time in stillness. To share the insights you have been given. To seek direction in the wisdom of the ancients. Decide whether you need to find a soul friend to be your guide.

PRAY Throughout the day make areas of silence and say, 'Speak, Lord, for your servant is listening.'

3 Pray.

> Awaken me, Lord, to your presence
> Open my ears to your call.
> Awaken me, Lord, to your presence
> Open my eyes to your coming.
> Awaken me, Lord, to your presence
> Open my heart to your love.

2
Lindisfarne Learning

These monks were strange men. During the darkness of that first night Chad had been rudely awakened and made to understand it was time for church. Immediately, as he rubbed his eyes, he heard the calling bell. Outside it was pitch dark with a sky full of stars. The church was cold and he shivered. He could not remember how long the service was but it appeared to be quite short and he was soon back into his bed; the covering had not had time to get completely cold. Chad was sure he had not been asleep for long when he was called again, for yet another short spell in the church. He was certain he would need to lie in when the morning came. But there was to be no chance to stay in bed. After another service, which was the Mass, it was time for work.

Today there were other huts to build, as the arrival of the four brothers had caused a shortage of room. Already two monks were driving birch poles into the ground. They were working parallel to each other, and only a foot apart. Two other monks were holding the posts. It was decided that this was a good job for the young boys. Poles were being placed about three feet apart and the rows only a foot apart, so everyone was working closely together. The monks, on makeshift ladders, were hammering away, otherwise there was little sound.

Chad felt uneasy holding the pole whilst the large hammer was being swung overhead; every time the hammer hit the pole it made him shudder. It also hurt his hands, yet he dared not complain. Other monks arrived with green hazel and willow. They sat down and showed the other two boys how to make hurdles. After a while Chad also got the opportunity to weave withy hurdles. He learnt that it was important to go regularly over and under the uprights with the smaller branches to give the whole hurdle stability and strength. Whilst doing this, he realized that it was the same weaving pattern he had seen at home as he had watched his mother and sisters working the loom. This working at house building lasted until noon and was then interrupted by the ringing of the bell and the call to worship. Once again the words were almost familiar, and the boys took part in the Lord's Prayer and the Gloria at the end of each psalm, with Chad's piping voice heard a little behind the others. The boys could not take a full part in the service; they could only be there, but being there was important. Then they worked until three, until the bell for another short service, then it was time to eat. Chad was amazed how, as the day had gone by, he had forgotten about food and had joined in the work with the rest. Now, however, he felt he was starving. Never mind – he was in for a feast, or so he thought. He was to be disappointed for the food was much like the day before. True, there was a little fish instead of an egg, but the same hunk of bread and a little milk. He wondered how long he would be able to go on like this, yet all the monks looked as if they thrived on it: all of them were strong and muscular. Again he thought that slaves on his father's estate would be fed more often than this.

Not long after the meal it was time for church yet once more, and again the same rhythmic sounds. Chad did not listen to the words and was feeling tired. He could have lain down and slept. Cedd looked across at him and smiled and that was an encouragement. He could not see the face of Caelin but it looked as if Cynebil was trying to say some of the words. No doubt he was only moving his lips, for the words were strange to them all.

Back in the hut his soul friend said, 'It is now time for study. We have worshipped, we have worked, so now it is time to study and to meditate.' Chad was not sure what his companion was talking about and could feel his eyes closing yet again. 'We begin with Psalms. You will have to learn them, for without them you are not able to take part in our daily worship. You will have to learn them off by heart. You know the Psalms come from the Old Testament and are the Songs of David.' Chad nodded and then asked, 'How many are there?' He was wondering how quickly he would master them.

'There are one hundred and fifty of them.'

'Do I have to learn them all?' asked a tremulous little voice.

'All of them, for they are all used in worship. You will not be able to take a full part in the services until you have learnt the Psalms. Later you may learn to read them from a book, but we have only one such book here and you cannot use it. Anyhow you need to know the Psalms off by heart so that you can use them at any time. It is good to be able to say them when you are working or walking. There is yet another thing, you will have to learn the Psalms in Latin, for that is the language of the Church. You will have to learn them in Latin and yet know what they mean in your own language so that you can tell others. We should begin at the beginning with the first psalm. I will say a verse then see if you can repeat it; soon you will pick up the meaning of the words. "*Beatus vir, qui non abiit* . . ." And that is, Blessed is the man who has not walked in the counsel of the ungodly, nor stood in the way of sinners: and has not sat in the seat of the scornful. His delight is in the law of the Lord: and in this law he will exercise himself day and night.' The learning of the first two verses took most of the evening. Chad also discovered that this was the way they would spend many evenings. When this psalm was said three days later, all of the four brothers were able to recite it. Again Chad's piping voice was heard clearly above the others. There was a great delight shown by all that the brothers could take part.

For the days and weeks that followed, the same pattern of worship, work and study went on and on. Chad did not get a lot of time to talk to his brothers. The striking of the bell regulated every part of their waking day, and broke into their nights. It seemed that Cedd was making the most progress; of course, he was the oldest. Soon all of the psalms that were said each day were known, as were the short responses to the sentences said by the leader. Sometimes they sang the psalms but more often they were said. On Wednesdays and Fridays they continued their fast until three o' clock in the afternoon, though Chad was not sure any day was a feast day. Already in church the boys felt they were taking a full part, and were quite at home. In fact, when a new boy joined the group, they realized that they really had made some progress. Soon each of the monks had a boy to teach. Sometimes they sat on the beach facing the mainland, chanting by rote the next thing they were to learn; at other times it was only with their soul friend. Psalm-saying became like eating, part of their daily diet, and in its own way fed them.

In the evenings the young lads were expected to tell their soul friend of all their activities, and especially their failings, during the day. This was not so much a formal confession as an act of trust and a chance for some direction. The soul friend did not make his confession to them, but taught them something new each day. If it was not psalms and responses, it might be how to observe the phases of the moon and from that to calculate the tide. They would need to learn the relationship between moon and tides, for this would save them much time in their travelling to and from the island. A break from study was the opportunity to go out fishing. Chad was a little fearful at first; the sea was so deep and the boat seemed so small. He was amazed how it rode the waves, especially when it was under sail. A good catch of fish often meant a better meal in the refectory. When the salmon were running, or the mackerel and herring were to be caught, there was plenty of fish indeed. Stormy weather was always difficult for their boats could not cope with great waves. If a boat got broadside on to a wave it could so easily be capsized. The monks were excellent seamen and fishermen, yet in Chad's time at Lindisfarne more

27

than one group was lost at sea. The islands further out than Lindisfarne had some particularly bad currents. Fortunately the island also abounded in shellfish; it was easy to gather mussels, crabs and oysters. Then there were eggs to collect from the sea birds; there were lots of ducks so they were not short of ducks' or gulls' eggs. Some of the eggs had to be laid down for later in the year, and this was not always successful. Hens were kept on the little farm that was being established, as were a few cows and sheep. The farm was like theirs at home and soon all the boys were giving a hand at milking the sheep and the cows. Fields were cleared of scrub and sown with oats, barley and wheat. They were to discover that barley liked the island climate, so barley bread became part of their regular diet. The lads were learning to plant and sow, to reap and mow, as well as their psalms. There was carpentry to be done, nets to make or repair, cloth to weave and clothes to make. The monastery was becoming a regular little coastal village – apart from all the times they went to church. The bell-ringing and psalm-chanting gave a strange rhythm to all that they did. The daily services were Lauds, Prime, Terce, Sext and None, Vespers and Compline, and the Mass was said regularly. Within the first year the boys had not only learnt the Psalms in Latin but could take a full part in all the services. They became servers and readers; and later they were given their turn in leading the service and then taking the main part. There was a feeling that they were progressing; nothing stood still, they were ever moving quietly forward.

Now that worship was possible it was necessary

for the pupils to read Latin. Those who did not know their alphabet would need to learn that first. Often the lesson was on the little beach to the west of the church; the boys would be encouraged to write in the sand and to share their faith as well as their food. Soon talk of God, of His love in creation, in redemption and in sustaining all things, became quite natural. The boys were encouraged to pray to the Holy Trinity in their own words.

> The Father to love me.
> Christ to redeem me.
> Spirit to guide me.
> God up above me.
> Christ down beneath me.
> Spirit right within me.

Such statements became a game to play, and yet it was so important to their learning.

'I believe, O Christ, that you are...', one youth would say as he pointed. The one pointed at finished off the sentence: '...the King of kings and Lord of lords.' He then pointed saying, 'I believe, O Christ, that you are...' Chad, being pointed at, continued the sentence: '...the Bread of life.' Chad then pointed at Caelin and said as he pointed, 'I believe, O Christ, that you are...' Caelin replied, '...the true Vine.' Sometimes the boys would add a rhythm to this by clapping their hands with two loud claps as soon as someone said, 'I believe, O Christ, that you are...' Then after the claps the person would reply. Chad enjoyed making loud claps and in later life would use this to call the brothers to him. Cedd told Chad he could clap like thunder.

Usually in this learning game all the seven 'I am' statements by Jesus in St John's Gospel were used. The boys loved to bring it to a climax by '. . . the Resurrection and the Life', '. . . the Eternal Son of the Father', and ending with '. . . here and with us now.'

A deep friendship was growing throughout the whole community, and when brothers went out on mission they were greatly missed. A brother could be away for a few days or even a month. When they went on mission it was usually in twos, in the same way as Jesus had sent out his disciples. Chad fancied doing this. It must be exciting telling people of Jesus, baptizing Christians and helping to begin churches. He fancied going out, for he would like to leave the island for just a little time. When he asked his soul friend he got the strange reply, 'Not until you can fly on eagles' wings.' Seeing that Chad was completely at a loss, he continued, 'You need to learn a Gospel off by heart in the same way that you learnt the Psalms. You cannot go out on mission if you do not have the Gospel in your heart. Not only do you need to know the story, you need to know the Saviour. I said you need to fly on eagles' wings, because I think you should learn the Gospel according to St John. I know Mark is the shortest, but you could easily learn St John's Gospel.'

Chad, eager as ever, wanted to learn immediately: 'When can I start?'

'You can start today at the beginning,' said his soul friend with a twinkle in his eye. "In the beginning was the word". Now repeat that after me.'

Chad was going to learn quickly and he would soon be able to read it as well. It was time to practise the lettering of these words, so he was given a wax tablet by his soul friend. This was an exciting moment. The wooden holder of the wax had been carved with a Celtic pattern around the edges, the inner square scooped out to hold the wax. Chad also like the look of it, for it looked like a short sword. He was beginning to acquire the weapons of a warrior. By word and prayer he would seek to defeat the powers of evil. He learnt that 'the word of God is sharper than a two-edged sword.'

Over the next few months all of the brothers mastered reading and writing. They learnt the Gospel of John and so began to fly on eagles' wings. Along with John's Gospel they learnt the stories of the birth of Christ, the miracles and the parables from the other three Gospels. All of them helped to lead parts of the daily services as well as assisting at the communion. The exciting day came when Cedd was asked to go out on mission with Aidan. Chad wished it was him, but knew his turn would come.

Chad grew in stature and in wisdom. At the same time the little monastic community increased in size. Monks joined them from Iona and from Ireland. More houses were built and more students were then taken on. The Celtic-speaking monks learnt English and the English students learnt Latin as well as the Celtic tongue. Slowly but surely they moved out into the countryside, where many were eagerly awaiting them. By the time Chad went out on his first mission there were little churches or standing crosses in the centre of communities. There was a lovely church in the capital at Bamburgh. People stopped work and flocked to hear the

31

preachers with their bells which they struck to call all to worship. The preachers always travelled on foot unless compelled by necessity to ride. Whenever they met anyone on the road they stopped and spoke with them. If the people they met were already Christian they shared a time of prayer with them, and sought to inspire them to be generous and godly in their living. If the people were pagans they told them about the presence and the power of the blessed Trinity, urging them to be baptized. If on their travels they were given gifts by the rich, Aidan told them to give them away freely to the poor: 'As you have freely received, freely give.' Sometimes Aidan kept the money he was given until he had enough to buy a slave at the local market. The slave would then be offered his freedom, but if he had nowhere to go the slave would often end up at Lindisfarne as a free worker or as a student. So Chad and other well brought up students shared their learning and their hospitality with freed slaves, and they held all things in common with them.

The months turned into wonderful years. This was a time of growing in their devotion to their Lord, of increasing their faith and of learning to share it with others. Another exciting moment came when the brothers were offered the chance of becoming soul friends to new students: 'You know the Psalms and our daily services, you have the Gospel in your heart and mind, you have shared in mission. Above all you have shown that you are immersed in the presence of Father, Son and Holy Spirit, so you are ready to become an Elder. You have passed the first stage of wisdom, so you are ready to pass on what you have learnt to others. You will still need your soul friend, for a person without a soul friend is like a head without a body, but you in turn can be a soul friend to a young student and help him grow in the faith.'

As the years passed it was obvious that all four brothers were being prepared for mission beyond Lindisfarne. In the urgency of the times there was a great shortage of indigenous priests. Aidan wanted his ministers to be of the people: he wanted Angles, Saxons, British and a mixture of all of them. If they were to reach out beyond Northumbrian mission stations, monasteries would have to be built all down the coast and inland, and this would mean sending out the people he had already trained. Soon it would be time to split up the four brothers. Monasteries grew in number: Melrose, Coquet, Hartlepool, Sunderland, Whitby and Coldingham. Churches were arising in all major towns and in smaller villages. On many an Anglian farming estate a large wooden cross was erected for those who wanted to attend daily prayers. The perpetual problem was to find priests to minister to the ever-increasing congregations. The lay people were good at maintaining daily worship but they needed the sacraments. The supply of ordained men could not keep pace with the demand. The clergy were too thin on the ground, and expected to care for too many congregations. The distances covered by men from Lindisfarne were becoming too great. Yet priests needed proper training; they needed to learn how to preach the word and to be in line with the whole church – no one must be allowed to say whatever he liked. More priests were brought in from Ireland and Iona but the sooner local men could be ordained the better it would be. Aidan wanted it to be seen that the Church was not a foreign importation but belonged to the peoples of the land. Cedd, Caelin and Cynebil would all be ordained at Lindisfarne and sent out on mission. Chad, being younger, had more time, as ordination into the priesthood did not take place until a man was thirty years old. Chad would benefit by being sent to one of the older monasteries in Ireland for further study. In talking this over with Finan who was from Ireland and of the Clan O'Neil it was suggested that Aidan sent Chad to Rathmelsigi in the territory of the southern O'Neils.

EXERCISES

Bede says of Aidan, 'All who accompanied him, whether monks or lay folk, were required to meditate, that is either to read the Scriptures or learn the Psalms' (Bede, Book 3, Chapter 5, 1992).

1 Give praise to God with Psalm 145 verses 1–10, and see if you can learn the words.

I will exalt you, O God my King,
and bless your name for ever and ever.

Every day will I bless you
and praise your name for ever and ever.

Great is the Lord and greatly to be praised;
there is no end to his greatness.

One generation shall praise your works to another
and shall declare your power.

I will ponder the glorious splendour of your
    majesty
and all your marvellous works.

They shall speak of the might of your wondrous
    acts,
and I will tell of your greatness.

They shall publish the remembrance of your great
    goodness;
they shall sing of your righteous deeds.

The Lord is gracious and full of compassion,
slow to anger and of great kindness.

The Lord is loving to everyone
and his compassion is over all his works.

All your works praise you, O Lord,
and your faithful servants bless you.

2 *Teach yourself this creed and then extend it with*
   statements of your own.

> I believe, O Christ, that you are
> the Bread of Life.
> I believe, O Christ, that you are
> the Light of the World.
> I believe, O Christ, that you are
> the Door of the Sheep.
> I believe, O Christ, that you are
> the Good Shepherd.
> I believe, O Christ, that you are
> the True Vine.

I believe, O Christ, that you are
the Way, the Truth and the Life.
I believe, O Christ, that you are
the Resurrection and the Life.
I believe, O Christ, that you are
the Eternal Son of the Father.
I believe, O Christ, that you are
Here and with us now.

3 Seek to learn verses of Scripture and pray:

Blessed Lord, who has caused all holy Scriptures
    to be written for our learning;
Grant that we may in such wise hear them, read,
    mark, learn and inwardly digest them,
that by patience and comfort of thy holy Word,
    we may embrace and ever hold fast the
    blessed hope of everlasting life, which thou
    hast given us in our Saviour Jesus Christ.
    Amen.

(*The Book of Common Prayer*)

3

Journeying

Chad, being the youngest of the brothers, was an obvious candidate for further education. Now that he could read Latin and speak the Irish tongue, it was time for him to learn from the writings of the saints and great thinkers of the past. It would be good for Chad to learn a clear writing script and illumination from one of the great monasteries in Ireland. From the start it seems that the Anglo-Saxon monks had a special link with Rathmelsigi in what is now County Carlow. We do not know how Chad travelled to Ireland or who went with him. It is likely he took a short sea crossing. We can imagine him leaving Lindisfarne and travelling along the Devil's Causeway, the road that runs from Berwick-on-Tweed down to Hadrian's Wall; then it would be along the wall to Carlisle, perhaps with a pause at Banna which is the birthplace of St Patrick. Then there would be a journey down the Solway and along to Whithorn, the place of Ninian and the church dedicated to St Martin. From here it would be by boat to Ireland and Bangor which was founded by St Comgall. He would then travel on foot to Rathmelsigi, visiting other monastic settlements on the way. He would call at places like Monasterboice, Drogheda, Glendalough and Moone until he reached Rathmelsigi. He would discover the generosity of the Celtic monasteries and some of their great learning.

Chad felt like one of the travelling story-tellers of old, like a bard who would make his living by telling stories and handing down wisdom. He knew that all along his journey he would meet people who wanted to hear of Jesus and the Good News. People were looking for hope and for meaning to their lives. He thought of Aidan's words, 'Keep your feet on the ground and keep your life simple. Remember, the more that you carry around the more it will take up your time and energy. It is no use giving up material possessions and land to take on board complex ideas, piles of knowledge or intricate worship: keep it simple. Let the Lord speak for Himself, do not stand in His way, introduce people to Him and encourage them to form a relationship with their Lord.' Chad had been with Aidan often enough in the hills to put this into practice; now he would tell the story of salvation all along the road he travelled. Instinctively, Chad knew he would not be travelling alone, for his God was ever present.

Chad chose as his stopping-places a preaching cross, a church, a group of huts, or a farmsteading. He sat one night on a roughly made chair in a darkened room with a clay floor. Around him the floor had been strewn with straw for the people to sit on. The place was full and he did not feel very confident. Yet the expectancy on their faces drew something out of him. These hill people were yearning to hear someone tell a tale. 'Tell us of Lugh, who could walk on a bubble without bursting it,' said an ageing shepherd. 'That I cannot do,' said Chad, 'but I can tell you about the Holy One who walked on the waves in a storm.' He asked for stillness, until they could hear the wind.

'Now close your eyes and listen again. Can you hear the distant sea? Its roar is greater than the wind's roar and it can be heard for miles. The sea is mighty and its waves all-powerful. I have seen the sea destroy boats and men. I have seen the sea invade the shore and take away huts, boats and people. No one is as strong as the sea, no one except its Creator who is mightier. He stills the raging of the sea and the madness of peoples.'

There was something in the tone of Chad's voice; it filled the place with a resonance. Not one person moved. Here was the revealer of the Holy One. This man could see beyond the moors to the great sea, beyond the darkness to bright places. Chad continued his tale. 'The fishermen had left Jesus on the mountainside where He could be alone with God the Father of us all. About midnight, at the darkest hour, the moon was covered with cloud and the wind rose to a fury. In the boat the fishermen were in sore distress, wave upon wave was filling the boat and they were in fear of their lives. Jesus had noticed and He was concerned for each of them. He set off walking on the waves in the midst of the storm. He came with speed until He approached the boat. As you would expect, the fishermen were afraid when they saw Him among the waves: "It must be a ghost; no ordinary human can walk on the water. It must be a demon of the deep coming to take us down." Then Jesus called out to them, "Do not be afraid, it is I, Jesus, and I come to your aid."' Chad could see that every eye was upon him, all were caught up with the story. He went on to tell them of Peter sinking in the sea and Jesus rescuing him. He told them to think of Jesus, for if He was not a demon

41

or a ghost, who was He? Did they know that Jesus is God, the Son of the Father who created all things? Story-telling and challenge went on well into the night. He discovered these people were Christians of a sort, yet they had rarely seen a priest or heard the word of God. He found there were adults wanting to be baptized, and many longing to hear the Gospel story. He would have to stay longer into the night and tell the full Gospel and teach them to pray. Suddenly, towards the end of telling them of the crucifixion, a cock crew. It was time these people had some rest. Chad recited something he had learnt on Lindisfarne.

> As already in the darkness
> The cock does crow
> Heralding the new day,
> So in the dawning hour
> Let Christians sing,
> In the darkness
> To the coming light,
> To Him who comes
> The King of Might.

He then taught them a simple chant. '"Come, Lord. Come down. Come among us." Sing this each day at the dawning and again at its close. Know that God is with you always; the Lord never leaves you. He walks in your darkness and rescues you when you are in danger. Singing this reminds you that you are never alone. Now sing it over and over quietly as I extend the prayer.' Chad let them sing; it sounded like the rise and fall of the tide. After they had sung it about three or four times he began to speak over their singing.

Lord, I call upon you.
By the wounds of your body,
Lord, I call upon you, mighty Warrior.
By your fasting in the wilderness
By your loneliness upon the mountain
By your walking upon the sea
By your stilling of the storm
By your love deeper than the ocean
By your life defeating death
By your light dispelling darkness
By your power over the demons
Come, Lord, come near.
Come, Lord, come here.
Come among us.

At the end of this they could feel the air tingling in the darkness around them. Everyone waited in silence, half expecting the door to open and the Lord to enter. Chad reminded them: 'The Lord is here, His Spirit is with us.'

The journeying took longer than had been planned, because of the work on the way. There is no doubt that Chad earned his keep. Time and again he found little groups of believers. At Whithorn he found a monastery larger than Lindisfarne and a church built in stone. Here he noticed the vallum around the monastery and was delighted to see how circular it was. From Whithorn men were going across to Ireland to preach the Gospel. He was invited to stay there but he refused. Before he left he heard of St Ninian who had founded the church and monastery, long before Lindisfarne or Iona began. He went to the shore and looked out from the cave where Ninian used to go to pray, and saw a mountain in the sea. Chad thought it was

Ireland and hoped he would soon sail there. He was told it was the Island of Man and Ireland was further off. However, soon there was a group going to the monastery of Bangor; Chad could sail with them.

Bangor came as a shock to Chad. If Lindisfarne and Whithorn were towns, Bangor was truly a city of God. The great numbers of monks and the choirs took his breath away. Chad estimated that there must be nearly a thousand in each choir and there were three choirs. They told him that the Divine Praises never ceased in the churches of the monastery; as one choir finished worship another group took up the praises and there was perpetual prayer right around the clock. In the church, they had a light that was never allowed to go out, and certain of the brothers were responsible for keeping the flame burning. While he was there he learnt a new communion hymn called '*Veni Sancti*'.

Come, holy ones, take the body and the blood,
Drink the Holy Blood for you outpoured.
Saved by that body, sanctified by the blood,
Refreshed we give our thanks to the Lord.

Salvation's Giver, Christ God's only Son,
Offered for all, for the greatest and the least,
By the Cross and Blood victory won
He is the victim and He is the Priest.

Come, then, with faithful hearts sincere,
Receive salvation's guardian here.
He that rules the world, his servants shields
Christ, to all believers, life eternal yields.

Chad also heard about Comgall, the founder of Bangor. Comgall allowed his monks only one meal a day, and the discipline was very strict. Here were being trained great warriors for Christ; these were men of muscle and not just of spirit. All did some form of manual work to keep their feet firmly on the ground and their bodies in trim. A young monk said to Chad, 'If you do not have your feet on the ground you are no earthly use to the people you meet. We are not called to be angels but people of this world which God has given to us. The Church needs to show it's got muscle and body as well as spirit, or it will not get whole human beings.'

Another of the younger monks at Bangor had recently learnt the Rule of Comgall and was keen to share it with Chad. As they were working in the field the young man recited:

Keep the laws of the Lord:
Seek not to stray from them as long as you live,
and they will keep you from harm.
The main part of the Rule is, Love Christ, seek
   not to possess:
be devoted to the King and kindly to all peoples.

One of the smallest of the brothers, who could not have been much more than twelve, told him, 'Comgall said, "On the path of repentance do not be in too much haste; learn to advance one step at a time, do not try and rush like a charioteer."' Chad could not help but feel that there never had been a rush in his learning. He had studied for years and now he was in Ireland he was to learn more.

It was whilst at Bangor that Chad discovered the general climate of Ireland, wet and more wet. There were many bogs and saturated places. Chad felt that anything that could absorb water seemed to do so. There was a dampness in the air and on the ground; anything that could not stand the damp rotted away – and that included some people. Chad was told that the west coast was even wetter. Fortunately his journey was mainly down the eastern side. He must make his way to Rathmelsigi. This time it was not as a story-teller but as a guest of monasteries or farmhouses that he travelled. Each monastery made him welcome and offered him the use of books and of their learning. Soon he was aware that he had never seen so many books in his life. Nearly all the books were in Latin, though some were in Greek and a few in Hebrew. He stayed in cells that froze the occupants on cold nights. He met monks pale and thin through fasting or meagre diet, men who had worn their bodies out with austerities. Chad was certain that God loved them but he did wonder if that was what God required of them. He met men who had wrestled with demons and defeated them, who had fought great battles and won through the power of the cross. He met others who had been captivated by the Evil One and were demon-possessed. Time and again he heard murmuring like the sea, as monks or individuals chanted litanies such as:

> The Cross of Christ
> Protect us.
> The Cross of Christ
> Guide us.
> The Cross of Christ
> Save us.
> The Cross of Christ

Uplift us.
The Cross of Christ
Redeem us.
Christ of the Cross,
Christ of the Tree,
Have mercy upon us.
Mighty Saviour – forgive.
Holy Jesus – forgive.
Crucified Lord – forgive.
King of Life, protect us from evil.
Merciful Lord, protect us from evil.
Wonderful Saviour, protect us from evil.
Holy and Mighty One, protect us from evil.

In some places there was so much prayer the very
air seemed to tremble. There was much good land
and large tracts of the forest had been cleared.
There were herds of cattle, sheep and pigs but he
was to learn there were also times of *dochma more*,
of great scarcity. In the winter great snowfalls,
especially if early or late, could bring on famine.
Then there would be much rustling and thieving
and countless beggars on the road. Yet there was
hospitality of unbelievable generosity. People were
so willing to share what they had. On one farm
where he stayed he heard an old blind story-teller
saying, 'If the salmon were swimming in the river,
I'd give you one and share another. If a flock of
birds were to alight on the plain, I'd give you one
and share another. I would share my herbs and my
home, my vegetables and my fire.'

It was a great blessing to be able to read. Every
monastery had treasures to discover; there were
books from Rome, from Gaul, from Africa, from
Greece. In great books of vellum there were some

of the greatest thinkers the world had ever known all waiting to be met. The journey proved to be a great joy. Wherever Chad went he discovered not only a welcome but the presence and peace of God.

EXERCISES

They left their own country and retired to Ireland either for the sake of religious studies or to live a more ascetic life. In the course of time some dedicated themselves to the monastic life, while others preferred to travel around to the cells of various teachers and apply themselves to study. The Irish welcomed them all gladly, gave them their daily food, and also provided them with books to read and with instruction, without asking for any payment (Bede, Book 3, Chapter 27, 1992).

1 Psalm 139 verses 1–9.

Lord, you have searched me out and known me;
you know my sitting down and my rising up;
you discern my thoughts from afar.

You trace my journeys and my resting-places
and you are acquainted with all my ways.

Indeed, there is not a word on my lips,
but you, O Lord, know it altogether.

You press upon me behind and before
and lay your hand upon me.

Such knowledge is too wonderful for me;
it is so high that I cannot attain to it.
Where shall I go then from your Spirit?
where can I flee from your presence?

If I climb up to heaven, you are there;
if I make the grave my bed, you are there also.

If I take the wings of the morning
and dwell in the uttermost parts of the sea,

Even there your hand will lead me
and your right hand hold me fast.

2 READ Isaiah 43.1–2.

RUMINATE Chew over what this means: God is a
God who promises, protects and cares for us as
persons. He will not let us be overwhelmed or
burnt out: He will not leave us to be submerged or
melted down. In all your journeying through life,
your God goes with you.

REFLECT Think over what this means for you
personally. A perpetual presence. You are never
alone, you need not go it alone. In the midst of
your troubles God is present and He cares about
you personally.

RESOLVE to live by this knowledge and to seek to
be more aware of your God who never leaves you
nor forsakes you.

3 *Pray this ancient Irish prayer.*

The path I walk, Christ walks it.
May the land in which I am in be without sorrow.
May the Trinity protect me wherever I stay,
Father, Son and Holy Spirit.
Bright angels walk with me – dear presence – in
  every dealing.
In every dealing I pray them no one's poison
  ever reach me.
The ninefold people of heaven of holy cloud,
The tenth force of the stout earth,
Favourable company, they come with me, so
  that the Lord may not be angry with me.
May I arrive at every place, may I return home.
May the way in which I spend be a way without
  loss.
May every path before me be smooth, man
  woman and child welcome me.
A truly good journey!
Well does the fair Lord show me a course, a
  good path.

(Attributed to St Columba)

4
Rathmelsigi

When Chad first saw Rathmelsigi it was like finding a beautiful island in the ocean. After travelling
over bogs and through forests here was a great
clearing with fields and a settlement. On the outer
rim lived the *manaig*, those who farmed the land
and who married and had children. Children were
born into the monastic system; their families were
part of the larger monastic family. The *manaig* lived
between the world and the monastery and dealt
with both; they depended on the monastery for
livelihood and protection and in their turn farmed
the land. All in this outer enclosure were still in
earshot of the bell. In this area were the millers,
the bakers and the blacksmiths, the shoemakers,
as well as the farmers, shepherds and beekeepers.
There was at the edge of this area a kiln for drying
grain, a brew-house and the tannery for curing the
skins of sheep, goats, calves and cows. Many of the
monks worked daily in this area as well as the
manaig.

Rathmelsigi monastery was built near a secular
settlement and it was in the old enclosure or rath
of former times. The monks sought to live apart
from their neighbours but near enough to be of use.
The old enclosing wall was now grass-covered but
it was still very impressive and much more of a
proper defence than was the symbolic enclosure
of Lindisfarne. This wall was originally meant to

keep out ordinary mortals, not the power of evil; no doubt it was now used for the latter. At a guess Chad thought the earthwork had a diameter of about thirty-five men (sixty metres). Inside this enclosure were various buildings which would become familiar and which Chad was longing to explore. He could pick out the church and the oratories, the *Tech Mor*, that is the Great House where the monks ate; both the Great House and the church were about ten metres in length. Near the Great House were the kitchen, the guest house and the armarium where the books were kept. In the centre was a wonderful large stone standing cross, all intricately carved; as Chad stood before it, he recognized carvings of the disciples, and of the crucifixion with the angels. He guessed that the two men seated were Paul of Thebes and Antony of Egypt who were the founding fathers of monasticism. There were two strange fish carved and he did not recognize them as any he had seen. The interweaving pattern made Chad finger it. He felt how smooth the stone was, and realized what a wonderful piece of craftsmanship this sculpture was, especially as it was well over two men tall. The cross stood before the west end of the church. Chad was about to enter the church when he was welcomed by a group of young men and boys. He was made to feel at home immediately by the brothers; many were Saxons and some had even been to Lindisfarne. There was exchange of news and tales of the journey. Every newcomer got a chance to bring in messages from other monasteries and news of events on their way. The brothers wanted to know why Chad had come to Rathmelsigi, and if he could already read and write. Chad informed them that he was already able to read in Latin and that he could write with a fair hand. He had been a lector and a subdeacon whilst on Lindisfarne. He had come to Rathmelsigi because of its great library, to study the Scriptures and to learn fully the art of illumination. He hoped to become familiar with the early writers of the Church. He would learn the Computus, and so be able to make tables to calculate Easter. The young students looked on in awe, for this was no beginner but an elder already. He would be given a soul friend, so that he could pass on the knowledge that he had already received. In exchange he would be able to work with the manuscripts and books.

Chad found that living at Rathmelsigi was much like living at Lindisfarne, though he did miss the sea. There were the same daily offices and the same work around the monastery. Here he was told by the abbot, 'You will divide your work into three parts. There will be your own work, which will be the study of the early writers of the Church and the learning to write with a good decipherable hand. It will be to make quills and prepare vellum from the skins of goats, lambs and calves, learning to collect dyes from plants and lampblack from above the candles. Secondly, there will be the work of the place. This is how you will earn your keep, it may be on the farm or in the dairy, in the bakehouse or with the blacksmith. However, because of the *manaig*, our lay workers, you will be able to spend more time in study than you would in some places. We have students here from the age of seven to men in their early thirties. Thirdly, you will work for the good of others. This may involve mending someone's fence or repairing a torn garment; it may be teaching someone the Psalms or sharing your new-found wisdom. This work you will do for the love of God and your neighbour. Now, I will get someone to show you the church and the library, and of course where you can stay. There is an elder leaving tomorrow so you can have his hut. Tonight you will be looked after at the *hospitum*, with any other guests who have arrived today.'

Chad gasped at the size of the library. There were Gospel books and even a whole Bible, something he had never seen before. There were writings by the Early Fathers; names he would become familiar with included Jerome, Augustine, Hilary, Ambrose, Cassian, Eusebius. There were writings of Origen, the great genius of the Alexandrine school, and the works of Philo. There were books of laws, hymns, literature, classical poetry, even some folk stories and legends. Then there were books of geometry and mathematics; included with these were the Computus for working out the date of Easter. There were Easter cycles by Anatolius, Theophilus, Dionysius, Cyril and Augustine. There were books in languages Chad as yet did not know. There were books in the three holy languages, that is Latin, Greek and Hebrew. Most of the books had satchels made of leather to protect them from the elements. Some of them could only be used with special permission, and only those who could already read and write were permitted to use the library. Chad was told this was a place he would be allowed to work in.

On a practical level he was told that in the library and in his own cell there must be no piling up of rubbish; any scraps had to be carried out and the area swept clean with switches of birch. Dirt and the danger of fire were always to be guarded against when dealing with the library. In enclosures such as a monastery fire spreading from building to building was always a hazard to be feared like the plague. Too many books had been lost through a careless pile of rubbish and a candle falling over.

The main church was entered from the west end, smelling like most others of oakwood, honey wax, and earth. In this church were hangings and paintings of saints around the walls. The young man showing him around told him that the church was the centre of the rath and the centre of their life. It was a powerhouse and a special holy place, it was never to be treated lightly but always to be entered in awe and wonder. It was not like any other building and must never be treated as such. Even the church had parts more holy than others. The young man explained, 'There is the holy place, the holier place, and the most holy place. Into the holy place all can enter, including lay people; this is the main body of the church. Beyond the holy place is the holier place where only those ordained into the various orders of ministry can enter; this is the area of the altar and where the holy mysteries are celebrated. Beyond that', at this point the young man crossed himself before continuing, 'is the holiest of holies and it is for God alone. In this place lie the relics of the saints, the bones of our founder and his bell; his presence gives us a direct link with heaven. It is the relics of our father that helped to consecrate this place.' Chad was not sure of all the young man was telling him but the brightness of his eyes and the ardour of his words showed he not only believed every word but had absorbed it.

Outside the church this blond Saxon with a white tunic and a woollen hood suddenly said with a grin, 'Can you tell me what this is?'

> I came from the flowers of summer,
> I was carried on the finest wings.
> I became part of an ordered community
> Hidden from the eyes of men.
> I held sweetness that was to feed an army.
> I was taken from my makers' home.
> I was separated from my sweetness.
> I was boiled and boiled again in water.
> I cooled and became hard and reformed.
> I had a new straight centre to me.
> I gave out the light of summer in darker days.
> I am useful now in worship and burn to His
>   praise.

Chad did not want to interrupt the lad but he had heard such before. 'I know what it is, a candle.' The boy was a little disappointed that Chad got the answer so easily, but he was an elder already. With a jaunty step the lad took Chad around the perimeter of the rath and showed him the four crosses, one for each of the Evangelists. The cross in front of the church the youth called the 'Cross of Christ'. The Cross is the *axis mundi*, the centre of the world, and it is where heaven and earth meet.' The lad was going to expound what he believed but a bell sounded. Time for worship. Whenever the bell sounded all work stopped and all, no matter what they were engaged in, went to church.

Along with many others, who wore woollen cowls and simple tunics, they filed into the church.

There were no seats but the monks stood in rows, sometimes facing the altar and sometimes facing each other across the centre. Chad learnt later that even when they were facing each other, 'they had to look at God and not at each other'. The service was familiar, though a hymn was sung that Chad had not heard before. The singing was very manly and strong and done with a wonderful sense of rhythm. Chad looked forward to learning new hymns. As usual a long silence followed and no one made to move until the abbot left. Then all filed out to a building that was very similar to the church, the *Tech Mor*, the Great Hall. The food was similar to what he had been used to for these last years: barley bread, milk, eggs, fish, apples, nuts, cabbage and pulses and oat biscuits. They all shared in the preparing of the food, or at least in the bringing it in from the fields. There was not a murmur, for meals were in silence apart from the reading by the lector.

Often the reader introduced Chad to new saints and new ideas. This one started well, for the lector was reading the Life of Martin of Tour, by Sulpicius Severus. Chad listened with eagerness as he heard how Martin became a soldier for Christ. Another evening he heard how Martin gave half of his cloak to a beggar and in a vision later saw that the beggar was Christ himself. As he ate and listened Chad longed to be a *Miles Christi*, a soldier for Christ, and to lead a heroic life. As the weeks went on and his reading of books began in earnest whole new worlds were opened up to him. It was such a relief that so many of the saints were far from perfect, yet were great lovers of their Lord. Chad developed an urge to explore the very depths of his own soul and the world around him. He sought to understand the cycle of the moon and its influence on Easter; he knew from experience that in some way moon and tides coincided. There were other times when he longed to see his brothers. Once whilst in the scriptorium he wrote on a small piece of vellum:

How can I forget the radiance of Lindisfarne,
a place of such great and shining light,
the source of my vision and hope,
where the sun of faith rose out of the sea
And shone upon four growing brothers.

He wondered if he would ever set up a monastery, like Aidan, where there would be elders and learners. He wondered what he would make for a rule. They would be a community that sought to possess nothing, to covet nothing, to fear nothing. They would live close to the earth and be hospitable to all. They would live out the Gospel and so attract others to Christ. It would be exciting to establish communities where men and women could live in awareness of the presence and obey the will of God – communities that were free from corruption and violence, free from greed, and where all were accepted as equals. He began to write again: '*a Ri na rig, a Ri na run,* King of kings, King of mysteries . . .' He would have written a new verse but the bell rang. Chad wiped his pen and set off once more for the church.

During the meal that evening the lector was reading from Augustine and the words sounded a challenge to Chad: 'You weak things of the world, who have forsaken all to follow the Lord, go after Him, confound the mighty. Go after Him and shine in all the world.' After the meal Chad sought out the lector and read again the same words. That night he prayed to God that he might one day go out and shine in some dark place. Very often Chad used the lections in the evening to guide him to a new author.

From one of the Irish teachers Chad learned that he, like all people, was made up of the four elements. He got his soul from the air, his body from the earth, his blood from the water and his heat and colour from fire. He discovered that creation began on a Sunday in spring and the basic elements were created in the order of fire, air, water and earth. He recited, 'Earth is dry, water is moist, air is subtle, fire is hot'. He was surprised to learn that birds were created from water and not from air. Thunder was the elements battling against each other, especially fire and water. As he thought of storms, he uttered a prayer for travellers. Orion had now risen in the night sky so the onset of winter was near. The appearance of Orion usually ushered in violent storms on land and sea.

Latin grammar and Bible exegesis continued to be Chad's main studies. More and more monks were coming from Britain to study the Bible in Ireland. Chad's tutor insisted that careful observation of the world around must be used to balance all study of the Bible: 'Test it against what you hear and see; you are not asked for a blind acceptance.' His tutor was forever saying, 'Use all that you have – ears, lips, mind, heart and hands. Begin with the ears: he who does not have the capacity to listen will not learn. He who does not listen to others will not heed the voice of God. Be open, be attentive, be alert. Speak about what you have learnt. Repetition is important, it directs the mind and fixes good habits. With your lips affirm the presence. With your lips praise the Lord. Sing to the Lord, and when you feel you cannot say your prayers, sing them! Use your mind, it is far greater and more able than you can imagine. Learn to focus the mind on single things, especially when you are studying. The mind is able to concentrate in the most wonderful way, but it needs training. Image what you hear and what you are learning. Image what you are talking about to others. Imaging is so important. A mind without its pictures is dull. Learn to stop distractions by single words or sentences held in the mind.'

At this point the tutor recommended that they learnt from Cassian: 'Do all in love, keep your mind in your heart. You cannot comprehend God with your mind alone, you will need to use your heart. That which cannot be grasped by knowledge can be held in the heart. With your heart you will reach new levels; we are not here just for learning, we are here for adoration. Life is to be celebrated; over and above our work we need to rejoice and adore. Your mind will wander less if it is held in your heart. When all is done, and study and worship are in balance, set about some manual work. It is no use talking of heaven and ignoring the very world that God has given to us. Let your knowledge and your adoration be seen in the way you treat God's creation. Remember, he who hurts creation hurts himself. He who is not at one with his neighbour cannot be at one with God. Remember, obedience, even when it is against one's will, is the road to true humility. Be careful with food; let it not over-burden the body and so choke the spirit. At all times, affirm God is *i maig*, God is *i taig*, God is within, God is without. If you want to be at one with God, you have not to be divided in yourself: ears, lips, mind, heart and hands have to work as one. You cannot be at one with God and at war with your neighbour; there are too many divided and distorted people in our land.'

When Chad felt he was not living up to these high standards, he recited psalms and portions of Scripture, especially the Sermon on the Mount. A text that he loved dearly he had learnt from his *anamchara* on Lindisfarne and it literally helped him in many situations: 'I carried you on eagles' wings and brought you to myself' (Exodus 19.4). Chad knew that when he stumbled the Father upheld him; when he fell into the very depths the hands of God were there. The mission he was called to fulfil was God's, and God was ever before him, within and about him. For extra encouragement he went into the church and saw the Pascal flame burning – the flame of the risen Lord, the flame that told of his presence, the flame that burned the whole year from Easter until the following Good Friday. This light so often brightened Chad's life. He would say to himself some words of Augustine's: 'The Christian should be an alleluia from head to foot.' Chad would then pray Augustine's words: 'O love ever burning, and never extinguished, my God, set me on fire.'

The rhythm of worship, study, manual work, rest, became the pattern of weeks and months and years. Often he was called to share in the teaching of others. Very often he would read from a Gospel book with a student looking over his shoulder and

trying to follow each word. At first the news from
Lindisfarne was quite rare. Then came news that
delighted Chad. All his brothers had been priested;
now only Chad, because of his age, was not
priested. How proud their parents would have
been. Then came sad news: King Oswin of Deira
had been murdered, through the treachery of
Oswy. Even worse news followed from the same
messenger. Aidan had died on a visit to Bamburgh.
It was a student from Lindisfarne who brought this
news. He had been sent by Finan along wi h a few
others to learn at Rathmelsigi. Finan was the new
bishop and abbot of Lindisfarne in place of Aidan.
He was the son of the northern Ui Neil, high king
and brother of Fina the mother of Prince Aldfrith.
There would now be new links between Lindisfarne
and Ireland. Very soon it seemed that boat-loads
of students were coming over to Rathmelsigi, and
each brought news. Finan was building a new
church on Lindisfarne, one fit to be a cathedral.
Chad should have rejoiced, but the little church on
Lindisfarne was dear to him and part of his growing, and it was the church of Aidan.

The next news to arrive was good news; it was
of his brother Cedd. The year was 653, when the
pagan Penda, who had killed Oswald, allowed his
son Peada to marry the daughter of Oswy. However,
Oswy had made a condition of the marriage that
Peada become a Christian. Oswy himself told Peada
of Jesus Christ. When he was finished Peada said,
'I would accept the faith gladly even if I were not
to marry Alhflaed.' Peada was then baptized by
Bishop Finan at a church on the Roman wall at
Ad Murum. When Peada returned home to Mercia,

he took with him four missionary priests from Lindisfarne to work among the Middle Angles: they were Diuma, Adda, Betti and Cedd. Diuma, an Irishman, was made bishop of the Mercians. How wonderful that Cedd was in a real missionary situation. Chad longed to go and share with him.

In 655 visitors brought more news. It would seem that Oswy was as keen as ever to spread the faith; he saw Christianity as a way of bringing unity and peace to the whole of the land. This time it was Sigebert of the East Saxons who, on visiting Northumbria, was persuaded to accept the Christian faith. Once again Ad Murum was the place for a royal baptism and again Finan was the person to perform the sacrament. Sigebert also wanted missionary priests, and two were sent to Essex. Cedd, withdrawn from Mercia, was one of the two. This made Chad realize how short of priests they were in the areas that were becoming Christian, and he began to think he must return to his homeland. The messenger had kept the best part until last. 'To work with the East Saxons your brother Cedd saw that more priests were needed, so he went to Lindisfarne and asked Finan for help. It was not the help your brother expected. Cedd was consecrated by Finan. Cedd has been made a bishop. Already at Bradwell he has gathered a multitude of those who would give their lives to Christ. He has a monastery where they are living under the good discipline of his rule.'

Chad was overjoyed to think of his brother reaching out into what was pagan territory and bringing new believers to Christ. His own brother a bishop and the founder of a monastery. That night Chad could hardly sleep he was so full of happiness. Time and again he prayed for Cedd and his work, and he prayed for Caelin and Cynebil. He prayed that one day they might all work together to the glory of God.

The stream of students kept coming and new cells and buildings were erected at Rathmelsigi. Then in 659 came the news that really made Chad determined to return to work with his brothers. Caelin had become the chaplain to Ethelwald the king of Deira. The king wanted a monastery where he could go and pray, where in the end he would be buried and where the monks would continue to pray for him after his death. Caelin had introduced Ethelwald to his brother, Bishop Cedd. There was much excitement as they talked of a monastery not far from York, but far enough into the wilds and the hills. The monk of the seventh century still sought to have his monastery in borderlands near the desert, the sea or the wilderness. Cedd wanted a place of seclusion, though also of easy access to the centres of population and authority. He was given some land at the foothills of Blackamoor and there he had set up a monastery, at a place that was later to be called Lastingham. It would seem that while Cedd was fasting and praying for forty days, he was called away by the king. Cynebil took over and completed the fast. Chad jumped for joy. Here was news of the three of his brothers all at once; the only one not present was himself. He was all the more determined to go and work for Cedd, or should he say Bishop Cedd. He prayed, once more, for his brothers: 'Mighty God, defend them on every side, with your power and protection. Keep them safe in every pass, be a

66

shelter in every storm. Be with Bishop Cedd and the priests Cynebil and Caelin; may they abide in your presence and in your peace. Deliver each from the soles of their feet to the crown of their heads. Deliver them from disease and from the Evil One. Deliver them, O Lord, and keep them from harm. Give them the grace and the power to serve you always; through Christ our most glorious Lord.'

A young teenager called Egbert came from Lindisfarne. He was from a noble family and from the start was a keen student. Chad made friends with him and often talked of Lindisfarne and the daughter monastery at Melrose. Egbert loved reciting the Psalms, and said there was little more that one needed for a life of devotion than the Psalms. He said it would be good if one day Chad and he could take the story of Christ back to the land of their forefathers. Chad said it would be great, but secretly, in his heart, he longed to return to Northumbria. Yet when the time did come, Chad was sad to leave. Rathmelsigi had become his home. When the day came for him to depart, he visited the crosses of the evangelists and then stood before the cross of Christ. He knew he owed much to this place and to the brethren. But life is not a resting place, it is a road, and it was time to move on. As he left he looked back on Rathmelsigi and prayed.

Christ's cross over this place.
Christ's cross over each face.
Christ's cross upon the land.
Christ's cross guide each hand.
Christ's cross behind and before.

Christ's cross at every open door.
Christ's cross in hollow and hill.
Christ's cross shielding from ill.
Christ's cross on all by sin vexed.
Christ's cross for this world and the next.

At each sentence Chad made a sign of the cross over different parts of Rathmelsigi. He left by the cross of St John and never turned back.

As he walked, he thought upon what he had been taught at Rathmelsigi about martyrdom: 'There are three martyrdoms, the white, the red and the green. White martyrdom is when, for the love of God, you separate yourself from all that you love; this will involve fasting and hard work. Green martyrdom is when one controls one's deep desires by labour and fasting, not allowing oneself free rein but curbing the passions and the will. Not only does this involve discipline of body, mind and spirit, it will involve you in repentance and acts of penitence.' Chad decided he would return to Northumbria, but not seek to join his brothers unless summoned to do so. 'Red martyrdom is to endure the cross of destruction for Christ's sake.' Chad knew that this was not always death at the hands of others, but it could be dying in a storm at sea or from the plague whilst caring for ill people. Chad might have tried not to long for his brothers, but his heart yearned to be with them. It must be really exciting being the founders of new monasteries and to be there at the very beginning.

EXERCISES

Chad devoted himself to the practice of humility and temperance, and study (Bede, Book 3, Chapter 28, 1992).

1 Read Psalm 27 verses 1–7.

The Lord is my light and my salvation; whom
    then shall I fear?
the Lord is the strength of my life; of whom then
    shall I be afraid?

When evildoers came upon me to eat up my flesh,
it was they, my foes and my adversaries, who
    stumbled and fell.

Though an army should encamp against me,
yet my heart shall not be afraid;

And though war should rise up against me,
yet I will put my trust in him.

One thing have I asked of the Lord; one thing I
    seek;
that I may dwell in the house of the Lord all the
    days of my life;

To behold the fair beauty of the Lord
and to seek him in his temple.

For in the day of trouble he shall keep me safe in
    his shelter;
he shall hide me in the secrecy of his dwelling
    and set me high upon a rock.

2 Check over your life and see how balanced it is.

Is there time for worship and study, as well as work? A life that has no time for worship is a greatly impoverished life, no matter how many things we possess. We need to adore, or all life will come to nothing.

Do we reflect our faith in the way we deal with others? How we care for others is every bit a part of our meditation as our time in quiet. Often what we truly believe is revealed in our attitude to other people and to the world.

3 Pray this prayer of St Benedict.

Almighty God, give us wisdom to perceive
   you,
an intellect to understand you,
diligence to seek you,
patience to wait for you,
a vision to behold you,
A heart to meditate upon you,
and a life to proclaim you:
through Christ our Lord. Amen.

(St Benedict)

5

Lastingham

The year 664 was a memorable year. Not only was it the year of the Synod of Whitby, it was also one of the years when the plague decimated the population. On the first of May there was a total eclipse of the sun and people were saying that the end of the world was near. There was a smell of death in the air and hearts were fainting for fear. Communities were dying, and in some places whole villages were being wiped out leaving no one to bury the dead. This was a time when priests were badly needed. The dead were to be buried and the living were in such a state of shock or fear that they needed lots of attention. Priests and bishops were also dying. It would seem that after the Synod of Whitby, most of the participants caught the plague; bishops, abbots, monks and priests died or caught the wasting disease. Cedd did not escape, nor did the monastery at Lastingham. Cynebil was also ill. There was hardly a brother fit enough to look after those who were ill.

Cedd decided he needed more help. Two messengers were sent, one to Essex and another to Chad. Cedd requested that Chad come to look after Lastingham and be its abbot. A little later a second messenger was sent to Essex to tell them that their abbot had died. When it was known that Cedd had died, about thirty Saxon monks requested permission to go to Lastingham to be near their father in God. In true Celtic fashion they wanted to be near the body of their founding father. No doubt this was not a wise thing to do, for the plague was rife in the Lastingham community. Yet these men came and joined the brethren of Lastingham. For a little while the number of monks was at the highest it had ever been, but it was not long before all the monks from Essex had caught the plague and died or were dying. It was into this sad situation that Chad arrived.

Chad's journey was a harrowing one, for death seemed to be everywhere. He felt it was not a good time to leave where he was, but the call from his brother had sounded urgent, and as Cedd was a bishop Chad, by now a priest, needed to obey. Caring for desperate people on the way caused minor delays. Chad could not turn his back on the cries of the poor or the pleading of the fearful. As he travelled he brought peace and solace to many communities and people. He comforted the bereaved and committed the dead to the keeping of God.

It was November when Chad arrived at Lastingham. The moors looked black and the fog hung in the vale. The little streams that ran off the moors were full of brown peat-stained water. He had arrived too late; nearly the whole of the community had been wiped out, including two of his brothers. One of his first tasks was to visit the damp grassy graves of Cedd and Cynebil and then to say Mass for them and for all the other brothers who had died.

Memories flooded back about the times when his brothers were together on Lindisfarne. A deep calm settled over Chad as he thought of the harbour on Lindisfarne which was so often calm when storms were raging, and of how Lindisfarne radiated peace when all around was in turmoil. Chad remembered those wonderful days spent with Aidan when all the four brothers were growing into men. Now Chad himself was being called to be an abbot. He prayed, 'May Lastingham provide peace and a sanctuary for people in this troubled world. May Lastingham be a safe harbour for the distressed and storm-tossed.'

In the next few weeks, things only got worse. Everyone was ill, and soon there was no one able to attend the daily services except one little lad who had come with the monks from Essex, and even this lad was ill. Chad made sure that the boy had food and was clean; each day he said prayers that this little lad might be delivered. He had been called to take charge of a community but it was soon reduced to him and this young boy. Yet the boy knew the daily services and his little piping voice reminded Chad of his own beginning at Lindisfarne. At this stage Chad found it difficult not to lose heart, yet he and the boy were spared from the plague. 'Saved for a purpose,' he told the boy. A few of the monks who had come to Lastingham at its beginning seemed to be resistant to the plague; they were ill but seemed to have an extra strength to recover. The little lad went around telling them all that he had been saved from death by the prayers of the abbot Cedd in heaven. He was certain that it was the prayers of the holy abbot that had rescued him from the snares of the evil one. They all ought to ask Cedd to pray for them. 'Cedd is close to Jesus; let him pray for you.'

A moment of joy came when they had a baptism. The boy saved from the plague decided he had never been baptized. Chad was amazed at this, seeing the lad had been brought up amongst the monks of Essex. However, the boy was insistent. Once a few of the Lastingham brothers were recovered and fit to return to worship, the little lad was welcomed fully into the family of God. As Chad signed the boy with the cross there were tears in the eyes of many.

Days were spent in burying the dead and burning contaminated clothing, saying Masses for the departed. It did not seem right that his brothers were buried out there in the open; perhaps when life improved, if it ever did, he would find somewhere better for them. Words that he had learned at Rathmelsigi kept coming into his mind, words of hope and encouragement that helped to keep him going.

> All shall be Amen and Alleluia.
> We shall rest and we shall see
> we shall see and we shall know.
> We shall know and we shall love
> we shall love and we shall praise.
> Behold our end, which is no end.

These were words from that great African scholar Augustine of Hippo. Chad had given comfort and hope to many families and groups of people with these words. Now he was needing to make sure that he personally had really taken them to heart, and that he meant every word. Time and again he said to the community, 'Let not your hearts be troubled . . .' But these were troubled times and many were losing faith. It was necessary that, even in their weakness, the monks should care for the people and the congregations around them, sustaining them in their time of need.

Very soon, even amid their difficulties, Chad was going across the moors into the valleys that were rarely visited by anyone. It was said that this was 'an area of wild beasts or of people that lived like wild beasts', but most of the animals that Chad met on the moors were timid, and so were the people. If anything, they were afraid of strangers; however that did not stop them being hospitable. The moorland people were mainly of British stock, though in some of the valleys the Angles had settled. Chad found that many were already Christian and were visited by the monks from Whitby. There were little churches in quite a few of the villages, and preaching crosses in others. On the high moors there were still some stone circles from pagan times, and many standing stones, but few people now took any notice of these relics of the past. It seemed that everywhere Chad went people were longing to hear the Good News and to turn to Christ. It would be good when all these communities and villages had churches and priests to minister to them.

On his visits to the hill country Chad would often be away for a few days at a time. How he loved walking on these high moors when the snows had gone. The great sweeping moors reminded him of the sea, and from some of the highest points he could actually see the sea. This made him think back to Lindisfarne and the early days. There had been such high hopes for them all, and now the plague had carried so many away. Chad uttered a prayer for the departed and then prayed, 'Lord if I am necessary to your mission, deliver me from all evil and give me strength to do what you would have me do.'

News was rare. People were not moving around more than they needed to. The population was still being decimated. A message came that Bishop Tuda, who had been appointed in the place of Colman, the bishop who had returned to Ireland after the Synod of Whitby, had died of the plague. There was news that Wilfrid had been nominated to succeed Tuda by Oswy's son Alchfrith, who was ruling in Deira as the sub-king. It was interesting that Wilfrid would be centred at York rather than at Lindisfarne. There was a definite move of power and authority away from Lindisfarne and towards Canterbury and Rome. Chad felt there could soon be more trouble for the Lindisfarne mission. When he had some time, he planned to go and see Eata and Cuthbert, who were at Ripon and building up a new base for mission by the rivers Ure and Skell.

Chad was told that Wilfrid was insisting on what he called 'a proper three-bishop consecration' and had sought permission to go to Gaul. He did not think it right to be consecrated by British bishops. The might of the Bishop of Rome was growing, and the Church seemed determined to build an empire like that of the old Roman Empire. There was a lot of seizing of power and a determination to beat down any who did not agree with their authority. Sometimes it sounded far from Christian. At the Council of Arles it was declared: 'Whoever does not celebrate Easter with Rome does not eat of the body of the Lamb, but dragon's meat.' There was a definite power move by Rome and it suited Wilfrid who was an empire-builder. Wilfrid was a great authoritarian and loved power. Already he had his own army and retainers and lived like a king. It was not that Chad disliked Wilfrid but they stood for different kinds of mission. Wilfrid went in to conquer peoples and possess them for the Church; to build up a kingdom on earth. Chad was more gentle in his approach and sought to discover the Christ who was already in the other person that he went to meet. Chad did not want to possess anything, but only to let people discover the love and light of God in their lives.

Chad had heard of the events of the Synod of Whitby earlier in the year and felt that Wilfrid had abused the position he held. Whitby had been chosen for the Synod because it had a safe harbour and Hilda had founded a good teaching monastery there. The main issues were to be the dating of Easter and the shape of the tonsure, though in fact both these issues were less important than the desire to control. Oswy the king called the Synod because his own household was split in the keeping of Easter. Queen Eanfled and her priest Romanus were still in Lent whilst Oswy and his Celtic priest celebrated Easter. The king was feasting whilst the queen was still fasting.

On one side of the king gathered Agilbert, bishop of the West Saxons and the only bishop appointed by Rome available, with Agatho his chaplain, Romanus, James the Deacon, Oswy's son Alchfrith, and Wilfrid who had instructed Alchfrith in the faith. On the other side was Bishop Colman, Abbess Hilda and some of the monks from Lindisfarne, Whitby and Lastingham. Cedd was chosen to be the interpreter.

Oswy began the proceedings by saying that it was only right that those who served one God should observe one rule of life and not differ in the celebration of the holy sacraments. Seeing they all hoped for the one heavenly kingdom, they should be united in the traditions they followed. Oswy then invited Bishop Colman to speak.

Colman told of how he had received all that he taught from his superiors. He said they followed the example of St John the Evangelist, who had celebrated Easter in this way. After Colman had finished speaking everyone had expected Agilbert to speak. In fact, Oswy invited him to make his statements. Much to the surprise of everyone Agilbert said, 'I request that my disciple, the priest Wilfrid may speak on my behalf. He can explain our views in the English tongue better than I can.' The Lindisfarne monks were dismayed at this, but could not say so. They knew Wilfrid to be a very powerful and gifted speaker. Already the Roman party had scored a little victory.

Wilfrid began by calling the Picts and the Britons foolish in their bid to stand against the rest of the world in their keeping of Easter. He then spoke of St Peter and Rome, and how the rest of the Church throughout the world was keeping the same date for Easter. Wilfrid ended by saying that the Picts and Britons were out of touch with St John as well as St Peter.

Colman rose and spoke again, but he was no match for this silver-tongued orator. When Wilfrid replied, he ended by reminding his hearers that the Lord had said to Peter, 'You are the Peter, and on this rock I will build my Church and the gates of hell will not prevail against it, and I will give to you the keys of the kingdom of heaven.'

King Oswy then asked Colman if it were true

that the Lord said these words to Peter. 'It is true, O King,' replied Colman. The king then asked if such authority had been given to Columba. Colman could only answer, 'No such authority had been given.' The king, after a little more debate, said, 'Since Peter is the doorkeeper, I will not contradict him but obey his commands in everything to the best of my knowledge and ability.' The whole of the Synod was then asked to give their assent and agree with Rome. Wilfrid was triumphant. Colman left feeling humiliated and defeated. With the king in control, the Synod accepted the ways of the Church of Rome. It was not long after the Synod that Wilfrid was appointed Bishop of York and set out for Gaul.

Unknown to Chad in 665, Wilfrid was consecrated at Compiègne in Gaul by Agilbert, formerly Bishop of the West Saxons and now the new Bishop of Paris. At the consecration Agilbert was assisted by eleven other bishops in great splendour. Wilfrid was carried on a golden throne by his fellow bishops. Wilfrid remained in Gaul and there were no signs of him coming home to his new diocese. It seemed he was not particularly anxious about fulfilling his duties back at York.

Meanwhile, Northumbria was without a bishop and there was no one to consecrate the priests who were needed to care for the people. The Church, like the nation, was in a desperate state. Oswy wondered whether Wilfrid was ever going to return, and decided he could wait no longer. Oswy, as king, had made decisions about the Church in the past. Was it not he who had called the Synod of Whitby, and he who decided that the ways of the Church of Rome should be followed? Now the

Church badly needed pastoral oversight and a con-
secrator of priests; it seemed Wilfrid was not going
to return to Northumbria. Oswy sent for Chad.
Knowing Chad to be a holy and modest priest
who was well read in the Scriptures, Oswy said he
wanted Chad to be Bishop of York. The city of
York had not had a bishop since Paulinus had left
in 633. The appointment of a Bishop of York rather
than of Lindisfarne showed the movement was away
from the Celtic influence on the Northumbrian
church, even though Chad was the person chosen.
Chad, believing that the Church needed pastoral
oversight now, and in obedience to the king,
accepted the appointment. He set off in 665 for
the south of the country. There were no bishops in
the north to consecrate him. He felt it would be
good policy and an act of unity to go to Canterbury. Chad and his companion Eadhed rode as fast
as they could, but at all times had to consider their
horses. The latter part of the journey to Canterbury
was through a harrowing landscape. Death and
poverty were everywhere. There were so many
emaciated people, so many whose eyeballs and
skin had gone yellow. Wherever Chad and Eadhed
stayed there were signs of sickness, and for this
reason they often camped out in the open. Whenever possible they avoided towns. Perhaps it was
because they avoided groups of people that they
did not hear the news that the archbishop they
were going to meet had died. In fact Archbishop
Deusdedit had died in 664 and the person
appointed in his place, Bishop Wighard, had died
on his way to Rome. The Bishop of Rochester was
also dying. There was no archbishop; in reality there
were hardly any bishops in the whole country. The

only bishops canonically consecrated, that is the way Rome saw as proper, in the whole country were Wini, Bishop of the West Saxons and Boniface of Dunwich. Chad and Eadhed had travelled far enough already but had no choice; they set off for Winchester. Wini was ready to consecrate Chad but two more bishops were required and there was a time of waiting until two Celtic bishops were sought out from the west country and brought to Winchester. During this time Chad again gave thanks for his family and praised God that from one household could arise two priests and now two bishops.

The consecration was in the splendid new cathedral built by the kings Kynegils and Kenwalch. The service was very moving. Bishop Wini spoke of the need for dedicated men who would offer themselves wholeheartedly to God. The singing of the choir sounded quite heavenly, though Chad was so overcome that he was hardly aware of anything until the hands of the three bishops were laid upon him. He was now a bishop in the Church of God. The consecration might not have had all the splendour that was afforded Wilfrid in Gaul, but Chad was properly consecrated and was now ready to return to Northumbria.

When he returned to the north, Chad chose Lastingham as his base rather than the city of York. He began to visit the neighbouring churches and to see to the pastoral needs of the people. New priests were ordained, many from his own community. He continued to live as a Celtic monk in prayer, study and fasting. Whenever he met anyone he sought to know if they were Christian, and if not, if they would be prepared for the sacrament of baptism. For Chad it was natural to stop in the middle of a roadway and pray with a passer-by. Whenever possible he continued this work on foot. He noticed on his visits to Whitby how the monastery there seemed to be prospering. They had a cowherd called Caedmon who was able to communicate with the ordinary people. Chad loved to have his feet on the ground. Though he enjoyed riding, and had a good horse, he preferred to walk. It was a joy to him, covering his great diocese and travelling through forests and over moorland. The road over Blackamoor had become quite familiar to him; he loved it at the time of the heather blooming. From the top of that moor he felt he could see over half his diocese. As he descended its lower southern slopes he always looked forward to a little more time at Lastingham. The church throughout the diocese was beginning to be rebuilt: new Christians were being made and new communities of worshippers spreading throughout the whole of the area. All over the area churches were being built and dedicated.

In the same year that Chad was consecrated, Wilfrid returned to Northumbria. Discovering that Chad was Bishop of York and not wanting to offend King Oswy, especially as there was no archbishop, Wilfrid took up residence in Ripon. Wilfrid's arrival at Ripon meant that the Celtic monks there had to leave, and this sent Cuthbert and Eata back to Melrose. Wilfrid would remain at Ripon for the next three years, though in that time he was for a good while in Kent standing in for the archbishop elect.

In 669 the new Archbishop of Canterbury, Theodore of Tarsus, arrived and immediately started to visit the whole of the Church that was under his jurisdiction. When he came to York he decided that it was Wilfrid who was the rightful bishop and that Chad's consecration was irregular. Theodore knew he had to make a strong stand and show his authority. On meeting Chad, Theodore pointed out that the two British bishops sharing in Chad's consecration were not recognized by Rome. Theodore even expressed some doubt about Bishop Wini. Added to this, there could not be two Bishops of York at the same time. As Wilfrid had been duly appointed and consecrated before Chad took up office, Chad had no right to be appointed. Theodore demanded that Chad step down and that Wilfrid be recognized as the rightful Bishop of York. This was not a request but an order, though if Chad had stood his ground there could have been an interesting battle of power.

Chad had laboured through the plague-ridden years, and worked hard to build up the diocese, to restore churches and to reach out in mission. He could have objected to the approach of Theodore and have pointed out that there had been no bishop anywhere in the north when he was appointed; in fact there was hardly a bishop in the whole of the country. Was Theodore saying that no Celtic bishops were proper bishops? Obviously, Wini did not think that way or he would not have involved them in the consecration of Chad. The authoritarian approach of Theodore could well have caused a new rift in the Church, as Augustine had done with the Celtic bishops. Chad was a man who practised humility; he did not particularly want a high position, and he would gladly step down. He said to Theodore, 'If you consider my consecration as bishop to be irregular, I will willingly resign from the office, for I have never thought myself worthy of it. Although I was unworthy I accepted it in obedience to my higher authorities.'

Theodore had expected more of a conflict and was taken aback by the humility of this saintly man. He would obviously be a good man to use in the Church, but it was necessary that he, Theodore, showed who was in charge of the Church. As Archbishop of Canterbury it was he who would say who were made bishops and who were not. It was not good to let the kings appoint their own men as bishops. It would be better to keep people like Chad on his side. Theodore carefully asked Chad if he would consider being re-consecrated with the requisite number of bishops and according to the Roman rite. Again, because he was a humble man, Chad assented to this. After his re-consecration, Chad returned to Lastingham. Wilfrid, as Bishop of York, was not far away in the city of York.

As a reminder Theodore later wrote into his 'Penitentials': 'Those who have been ordained by bishops of the Scots (Irish) or Britons, who are not Catholics in the matter of Easter and the tonsure, have not been united to the Church, but are to be again validly confirmed by the imposition of hands of a Catholic bishop.' Theodore would remain adamant on this and believed that there was something lacking in all the holy orders conferred by Celtic bishops. So when Chad was re-consecrated as bishop, Theodore began by laying hands on him for a re-confirmation of him in all his orders within the Church, as a sub-deacon, deacon and priest as well as bishop. Chad submitted to this in all humility, not for his own sake but for the unity and well-being of the Church. Theodore had no authority to make these demands and was relieved at the willingness of Chad to co-operate. Now that this confirmation of Chad had taken place, perhaps Theodore could use such a humble and obedient bishop. Chad returned to Lastingham as abbot and continued to care for the brethren. His first task was to persuade one or two of them that he had done the right thing in allowing Theodore to re-consecrate him.

EXERCISES

Chad devoted himself to keeping the Church in truth and purity, to the practice of humility and temperance, and to study. He visited cities and country districts, towns, houses and strongholds, preaching the Gospel, travelling not on horseback but on foot after the apostolic example . . . He was one of Aidan's disciples and sought to instruct his hearers in the ways of his master and his brother Cedd (Bede, Book 3, Chapter 28, 1992).

1 Read and learn Psalm 42 verses 1–7.

As the deer longs for the water-brooks,
so longs my soul for you, O God.

My soul is athirst for God, athirst for the living
God;
when shall I come to appear before the presence
of God?

My tears have been my food day and night,
while all day long they say to me, 'Where now is
   your God?'

I pour out my soul when I think on these things:
how I went with the multitude and led them into
   the house of God,

With the voice of praise and thanksgiving,
among those who keep holy day.

Why are you so full of heaviness, O my soul?
and why are you so disquieted with me?

Put your trust in God; for I will yet give thanks
   to him,
who is the help of my countenance, and my God.

2 *Can you join with the third-century Eusebius
   and say:*

May I be no man's enemy and may I be the
   friend of that which is eternal and abides.
May I never quarrel with those nearest to me:
   and if I do may I be reconciled quickly.
May I love, seek, and attain only that which is
   good.
May I wish for all men's happiness and envy
   none.
May I never rejoice in the ill-fortune of one who
   has wronged me . . .
May I win no victory that harms either me or my
   opponent.
May I reconcile friends who are angry with one
   another.

May I, to the extent of my power, give all needful
help to my friends and all who are in want.
May I never fail a friend in danger.
When visiting those in grief, may I be able by
gentle and healing words to soften their pain.
May I respect myself.
May I always keep tame that which rages within
me.
May I accustom myself to be gentle, and never
be angry with people.

3 Affirm.

I reach out in love towards God and His love.
I reach out in love towards God and His grace.
I reach out in love towards God and His power.
I reach out in love towards God and His purpose.
I reach out in love towards all who come to me.
I reach out in love in openness and friendship.
I reach out in love in kindness and forgiveness.
I reach out in love to my neighbour and meet
God.

6
Owini

Lastingham continued to attract more members to its community. The Church was almost the only place where the poor had an opportunity of improving their lot and holding a position of authority. To be a monk was also a way of avoiding being called up to take arms for any local battles. The monastic life did attract some who were seeking to escape, though life was far from easy and any who did not work or were not willing to offer themselves fully to God were soon weeded out again. There is no escaping from responsibility, from each other or from God, in a small community.

One day a man came to join the monastery who said his name was Owini. He was dressed in rough clothes, wore a deep leather belt and carried an adze and an axe. He was obviously a man of bearing and of great physical power. He did not look like the type of man to pick an argument with. Though he looked poorly dressed his actual whole being spoke of nobility. Owini was a man with an interesting past and an interesting approach to his own future. Chad met him and listened to his story. 'I was born into an aristocratic family; we were friends of the royal household of East Anglia. Early in my life I entered into royal service and worked my way through various offices until I became governor and head of the royal household. I was responsible to Princess Etheldreda.' At this point

Owini paused and said with some feeling, 'Such a noble and handsome woman and a wonderful Christian.' He then continued, 'She was married to Tonbert but he died shortly after their marriage. She then decided to become a nun, but it was not to be. In royal households, marriage is a good way to join in alliance with another kingdom. Etheldreda was told that she had to marry Egfrith of North-umbria. She was greatly disturbed when told this and asked me if I would travel north with her. She wept for much of the journey as she wanted to be a nun and not to marry. I wept too when I saw the child she was to marry, for Egfrith was only twelve years old, and not mature at that! Etheldreda was already twenty-five years old; she could have almost been his mother. At this early stage there was not much trouble. The boy would rather be out with other boys and with the hounds. It was not difficult for Etheldreda to remain a virgin for Christ. She took to wearing coarse clothes under her outer wear as an expression of her desire to renounce all wealth and become a nun. I was often in her confidence at the early stage. We said the daily offices together as if we were in a monastery. Time and again she said how she wanted to renounce all that she had and become a nun. The dear lady inspired me to give away all my pos-sessions and become a monk. Too often I saw the wrangling of the royal court for power, and the manoeuvres of Bishop Wilfrid. I did not want to have any part in this. As the years passed Egfrith grew into a man and desired his marriage to be consummated. Etheldreda refused, and in this she had the support of Wilfrid. He suggested she be allowed to join Oswy's sister Ebba at the monastery at Coldingham. Egfrith refused to listen and life became difficult. It was at this point that Etheldreda encouraged me to leave and seek out a monastic house. She knew I was out of favour with Egfrith and not really welcomed by Wilfrid. So I changed into the clothes of a labourer. I left all that I had for the benefit of the poor. I made my way here as I want to follow the old traditions, and I want to labour for Christ. I do not want to deal with books or writing. I already know the Psalms and the daily services. I beg you that you allow me to join you here at Lastingham.'

Chad was overjoyed at such a sincere and dedicated man. Owini would be an asset to any community. At the moment they were short of men who wanted to work with their hands. Owini would be just what they needed. He could look after the crops and their vegetable plot. He could teach other monks the value of manual labour. 'Owini, I welcome you in the name of the Lord. I will introduce you to the brethren after our next service. They will be delighted to hear that you want to worship God through your physical labours. It will be good for some of the young men to see that an adze, an axe or a hoe can lead to sanctification as much as poring over a book or even a sacred text. We need people to know that those who till the fields are as much part of the consecration as those who raise the sacred host. Those who reap share in the elevation of the bread as much as the priest. It is the presence of God in all places that gives significance to the labourer among the weeds and uplifts the bowed head.'

Owini responded by saying, 'I often feel like Jacob when I am in the field; I am wrestling with an unknown power. I end up by adoring among that with which I was struggling. There is something wonderful about the earth in the way it will repay a man for hard work. I feel that God speaks to me as I dig with the spade or use the adze. He is there in my labours.'

Chad replied, 'It would be good if more people discovered that the earth is still full of the glory of God. God has not left His creation and He is still to be found within it. When I was in Ireland I learnt that there are three groups of Scriptures. There is the New Testament, and to understand it fully you need to have some knowledge of the Old Testament. The Old Testament can only be understood if you have some knowledge of the Primary Scriptures. These Primary Scriptures are what we call creation. A person who is out of touch with creation and what is around them cannot grasp the true meaning of the Scriptures. If most people cannot find their sanctification through their work, they will not be able to find it elsewhere.'

Over the next few weeks Owini thought over these words again and again. 'God speaks through His creation, His voice is heard in all the world.' He prayed.

Let the hardness of the earth strengthen me.
As I develop the land, let it develop me.
As I pour my energies into the earth,
let it encourage my growth and resurrection.
Let me make contact with God through
   the earth,
through growing things, through the seasons,

94

through the patterns of death and resurrection.
As I am formed of the earth, let me respect my
forebears.

All who met Owini recognized that he had a deep
sense of the presence, the power and the peace of
God in his life. He was a joy to work with. He was
a man in tune with himself, the world and his
God. In Owini, God's world was affirmed and
honoured; you had to be gentle with the earth in
your dealings and learn to co-operate with it. One
day he was teaching a young man to use the adze.
The lad was putting great effort into it but the
wood he was hacking at was being torn into
pieces. He was swinging the adze as he was told,
but making no progress. The wood was becoming
rougher rather than smoother. Owini, standing at
the other end of the planking, gently swung his
own adze and the wood became smooth. He was
quietly teaching the boy a lesson, a lesson without
words. Now it was time to speak. 'Come, my friend,
and learn one of the secrets of the world.' He
brought the lad to the end he was working at and
asked him to try again. This time it was so easy, the
adze smoothed the wood. Soon the lad had made
quite a good job of the plank for a beginner. 'Now
let that be a lesson to you. It matters where you
start from and which direction you go. Learn that
wood has a grain and you must co-operate with it.
If you go against the grain it will never become
smooth. My boy, learn that this is true in all of life:
if you go against the grain it is no use asking God
for a smooth path before you. Learn to co-operate
with nature, learn to co-operate with the laws of
God. If you go against them you will end up in

trouble.' To watch Owini using an axe or an adze was a joy, and others could see the pleasure he got out of his work. Any wood that Owini adzed had a wonderful feeling of flowing smoothness to it; the wood itself felt quite sensuous.

Owini became one of Chad's dearest companions in a very short time. If there was hard work to be done, Owini was there. If there were heavy loads to move, Owini was ready to help. It was good to see the rhythmic swing he made with axe or adze, and the steady progress he made with the spade. Owini said that all he did, he did to the glory of God. He would say to the young men working with him, 'The easiest way and the oldest way to make contact with God is through a sensitivity to the earth. God speaks to us through His creation, through the earth, the sky, the birds and all His creatures. Learn the mystery of life by looking at growing things, and never lose a sense of awe. It is through this sensitivity and awe that God approaches us.'

Chad would point to Owini and say, 'Look, there is a man content with the world and with his God.'

EXERCISES

Owini decided to renounce the world and this he did in no half-hearted way: he stripped himself so completely of his worldly possessions that he left all that he had and, dressed only in a plain garment and carrying an axe and an adze in his hands, he came to the most reverent father's monastery at Lastingham. He did this to show he did not come for sake of ease, but to work hard. (Bede, Book 4, Chapter 3, 1992).

1 Read Psalm 8 and give thanks for the world.

O Lord our governor,
how exalted is your name in all the world!

Out of the mouths of infants and children
your majesty is praised above the heavens.

You have set up a stronghold against your
    adversaries,
to quell the enemy and the avenger.

When I consider your heavens, the work of
    your fingers,
the moon and the stars you have set in their
    courses,

What are mortals, that you should be mindful
    of them?
mere human beings, that you should seek
    them out?

You have made them little lower than the angels;
you adorn them with glory and honour.

You give them mastery over the works of
    your hands;
and put all things under their feet,

All sheep and oxen,
even the wild beasts of the field.

The birds of the air, the fish of the sea,
and whatsoever walks in the paths of the sea.

O Lord our governor,
how exalted is your name in all the world!

2 Think on these words by Evelyn Underhill.

To elude nature, to refuse her friendship, and attempt to leap the river of life in the hope of finding God on the other side, is the common error of a perverted mysticality . . . You are to begin with that first form of contemplation which the old mystics sometimes called the 'discovery of God in His creatures.'

(Practical Mysticism, 1943)

3 Pray.

Bless to me, O God,
The earth beneath my foot.
Bless to me, O God,
The path whereon I go.
Bless to me, O God,
The thing of my desire.
Thou Evermore of evermore,
Bless Thou to me my rest.

Bless to me the thing
Whereon is set my mind.
Bless to me the thing
Whereon is set my love.
Bless to me the thing
Whereon is set my hope,
O Thou King of kings,
Bless Thou to me mine eye!

(Carmina Gadelica, 1976)

7
Bishop of Mercia

In the same year that Chad was deprived of his diocese, Bishop Jaruman of Mercia died. This was the opportunity to remove Chad from the diocese of Wilfrid and for Theodore to show a friendship towards a Celtic-trained monk. Chad was obviously popular in the York area and this was not good for Bishop Wilfrid. Theodore and Wilfrid met with Wulfhere the king of Mercia and told him of the hard work and the saintly qualities of Chad. It would greatly please them if Chad could be offered the bishopric. A greater difficulty was to approach Oswy for permission to move Chad from the kingdom of Northumbria, but statesmen like Theodore and Wilfrid found a way, and Chad was appointed Bishop of Mercia. It is interesting to note that at this stage the kings had much say in church appointments and affairs.

It pleased Chad to go where his brother had worked as a missionary and where the Lindisfarne monk Diuma had been the first bishop. It made Chad think of the days gone by when Aidan was teaching and Diuma was at Lindisfarne. He would be a link with them, though he was to be the fifth Bishop of Mercia in such a short number of years.

The diocese stretched from the North Sea across to the river Severn. The population of North Mercia was estimated to be about 7,000 families, South

Mercia had about 5,000 families, a further 7,000 families were in the area of Lindsey. The base of this large diocese had been Repton. At Repton there was a large church and a double monastery in the Celtic style, ruled by an abbess. Chad worked from there for a short while but longed to found his own monastery, and at a site more central to his new diocese. He wanted a place where his own monks could both worship and be sent out in mission. He also wanted a place that had been hallowed by saints of old, if that were possible. On a practical level it was also where two great roads met, Watling Street and Ryknield Street.

At Lichfield he found a church dedicated to St Mary the Virgin. He heard an ancient story that it was here that a thousand Christians had died during the persecutions. Lichfield meant the 'field of the dead'. Here ordinary men and women had given their lives for their faith; they were holy martyrs. Here was a place sanctified by the blood of the saints. For a moment he remembered that Lindisfarne had been sanctified by the blood of the Christian king Urien ap Rheged. Here at Lichfield he would have his monastery and base. Wherever someone has fully dedicated their life, or died for the faith, that place is special forever.

Suddenly there was much to do. There was a protecting wall to be raised to encircle the site. There was a cathedral church to be built, houses for the monks, a hospice for guests, a refectory and a place that could be used like an island of quiet amid all the demands. The land itself had to have the basics of life: good soil and water. Before anything else the land had to be hallowed and claimed for the Blessed Trinity. The monks must show to all people that their priority was God Himself. They were called to worship and adore: 'You alone, Lord, do I seek. You alone I serve. You alone I follow.' Words came into Chad's mind from what he had learned at Rathmelsigi. We must show that we are on this earth to give glory to God.

Because it was said that on this very land Christians had died during the persecutions, the land would have to be cleansed of its past and prepared for its future. There was much to do, but it must begin with prayer. Though Chad had not been asked to consecrate a monastic site before, he knew what was required of him. He had heard Aidan speaking of forty days of prayer and fasting before any building was done. He had been told how Cedd had prepared the site at Lastingham and how his other brother Caelin had assisted. Forty days of prayer and fasting, hallowing themselves and the land, setting themselves aside as well as the earth beneath them – it was a time for consecrating themselves and the whole of the monastic site. This was a time when visions and dreams were allowed some priority. Into the forty days would be built plans and hopes for the future. Owini would find the stillness of these days difficult but it would be good for him, as he so often laboured too hard. Later he could clear the land and raise the vallum as his share in adoration. To the east of the present cathedral, Chad built his monastery on a small plot of land. Chad used a prayer similar to the one used by Aidan on Lindisfarne, and by Cedd at Lastingham. It was a prayer that looked in each direction and affirmed the presence and power of God.

God is before us
God is behind us
God's love around us,
On our right and our left.
God there above us
God there beneath us
God's might around us,
On our right and our left.
God all about us
God deep within us
God's peace be with us,
Today and forever.

Prayers like this were said over and over each day of the preparation, with the brothers joining in. Owini was allowed to mark with a spade the extent of the monastic enclosure. Chad gave each quarter his blessing. Within this enclosure would be the world in microcosm. They prayed that it would be a world renewed and restored. Within this space was an attempt at paradise regained. It was not with the foolish notion that they could keep evil out, rather with the prayer that goodness would triumph within. Here people would be able to come for peace, for healing, for renewal. The invisible walls would be a protection against violence and the power of the evil one. The gateways were meant to be gateways into the kingdom of God. Any who entered here would find mercy and protection. Crosses would be placed at the gateways as pointers to heaven and as a defence against the evil one. Some days, the prayer of dedication would be extended and acted out to emphasize that the whole site belonged to God, as does all time and space. It was not that some places did not belong to God, but through use and expectation certain places spoke more strongly than others.

Chad faced the sun as it rose and said, 'God goes before me. Into the building up of this holy place, into the future of the diocese, into the ages to come, God goes before me. There is no place I cannot meet Him, for He is there; there is no event in my life that is without His presence. The future is all unknown, but we know who goes before us and He is there to welcome and greet us. We may not know what lies ahead but we know Whom, for God goes before us.

'God is behind us, as our rearguard protecting us from attack and protecting us from the past. Places, like people, carry traces of what has been, and they can reverberate in our lives. The past needs redeeming if we are to live wholesome lives. We all carry memories and hurts that need the healing touch of our God. The land needs freeing from the violence and troubles of the past. The land, like people, needs hallowing. God's love is around us, on our right and our left. Let us and the land reveal the love of God.

'God there above us. The transcendent and holy God is above us and beyond us. We cannot contain Him by building walls or churches, but we can keep Him in our hearts. The God who is above the troubles and calamities of this world, but who comes to us in the midst of them, this is the God who uplifts us, who restores us and who gives us life eternal. The God above us is the God who came down in the Word made flesh to dwell among us. God, the heaven of heavens cannot contain you, but you are willing to be held in our hearts and as you come down you lift us up.' Chad thought upon some words of St Augustine at this point.

> Come, Lord Jesus, do not delay.
> Come, Lord Jesus, do not tarry.
> Come, Lord Jesus, draw near.
> Come, Lord Jesus, come in peace.
> Come as our Saviour,
> Come, desire of all,
> Come, show your face.
> Come, and we shall be saved.
>
> (St Augustine)

In response to this prayer, the monks were encouraged to say after each line: 'Come, Lord, come down, come in, come among us. 'Between each sentence there were long gaps as each and every one of them waited on the Lord who comes. They waited until He filled their very being. The Lord above came down and was made flesh among them.

'God there beneath us. The humble God who comes down to the lowest place, descends to hell and all the hells of our world. If we descend, He will be there also. If we fall into the dust, He is there also, and as He rises, He will rise with the dust clinging to Him, and we shall be saved. No matter how far we fall, or how often, our God is there and waiting; underneath are the everlasting arms, and the hands bear the print of the nails. All who come here will find support and hope, for we are in the very heart of God. Nothing can separate us from the love of God in Christ Jesus. Let all who are down come here, and be uplifted. Here the broken will be restored, and the weary will find new strength until they can soar like the eagle.

'God on our right and on our left. God in the height of the noonday, and in the darkness. God there in all our successes and in all our failures. God there in our joys and in our sorrows. Here let the successful rejoice, let the failures find courage, let the dextrous find joy, let the ham-fisted find encouragement. Let all, in the heights or in the depths, find God, and know his love.

> The Holy Three bless us.
> The Holy Three be over us.
> The Holy Three be under us.
> The Holy Three be all about us.
> The Holy Three be within us.
> And the blessing of the Three
> Be upon us, evermore and evermore.
> And the blessing of the Three
> Be upon us, evermore and evermore.'

The area vibrated with the Presence and with peace. All of creation was dedicated to Him who created it, to Him who redeemed it, and to the Spirit who sustained it. This hallowing was not to be taken away. It was to abide forever.

After the forty days, Owini came into his own, flexing his muscles and wielding axe or mattock, using splitting wedges and hammers. Now the building began. The smells took Chad back in time to the early days on Lindisfarne; it was the smell of oak wood, soil and greenery that filled the air day after day. The smell of the soil reminded Chad of a *Gloria* he had learnt in Ireland.

The earth,
The earth rejoices in you, O God.
The earth quivers with your praise.
The earth marvels before you.
The earth magnifies your Name.
The earth praises you, its creator.
Gloria . . . Gloria . . . GLORIA.

Chad gave glory to God for all who were coming forward to serve God in the monastic life. They were joining them at such a speed that it was hard to keep the building programme going. No doubt the plague had loosened the ties of many; they needed a place to live and the knowledge that they were loved. Others came in fear of death and judgement and had to learn to look at the God who gives life and who seeks that we have life in abundance. There were soon enough in the community for Chad to long for a little island like Aidan had had off Lindisfarne, a place to escape the busyness and to be still. Even a monastery can become a place of too much action. To this end another little dwelling site was prepared, and encircled, where Chad could go with about half a dozen of his brothers. Here they would wrestle alone with God, and seek renewal and new vision. On this site, as on the main site, out of necessity there was a well. This separate place was known as a Sunderland, or *Sundorwic*, a place sundered or separated from the rest.

The king Wulfhere gave Chad and his monastery fifty hides of land in a place called Adbarvae in Lincolnshire for yet another monastery. To such places Chad travelled and he preferred to travel as always on foot. He told fellow monks that he was no more important than they were and that he was not indispensable. If he did not make it to a place, someone else would go. This did not impress Archbishop Theodore, who did not think it fitting that a bishop of the Church should be wandering around like a poor priest or a peasant. Chad should act according to his status. Chad remembered that he had twice been made deacon – a servant. Surely to be a minister is not to be elevated but to come down in the world, just as the Christ came not to be served but to serve. Theodore, as Chad's superior, forbade him to travel on foot. If he was to leave his monastic city he was to go on horseback as was fitting for a bishop. Chad said nothing but obviously his looks said something. He was not pleased, but he was under authority and he would obey. It was whilst Theodore was still with Chad that Chad was to set off on a journey. He got his walking staff as was his habit, and was about to set off when he was confronted by a very imperious-looking Theodore. This was a matter of obedience. Chad had to ride, and to emphasize the fact Theodore forcibly lifted him on to the horse, saying, 'A holy man like you needs to obey his superior. I know you are getting older, as we all are; you must not think you can walk about as when you were a boy. I command you to ride.'

It was with mixed feelings that Chad rode off. He thought back to Aidan and the time when King Oswin had given Aidan a horse with all its royal trappings, a magnificent animal and worth a fortune. Aidan had felt uncomfortable with such wealth; it played on his conscience. The solution was soon found, for Aidan met a beggar in the road and gave away the king's gift. Needless to say, the king was far from amused. What would Theodore say if Chad gave his horse away? Chad chuckled at the thought, but knew he could not do that. Still, he said out loud, 'Aidan, I hope you will forgive me.' Chad certainly got around more on horseback and had to admit it was sensible.

Back at the monastery Chad, Owini and all the brethren stopped work at the sound of the bell. Their whole lives were made up of adoration and obedience, which was symbolized in this one action. No matter what they were doing or how important they thought it, when the bell rang they stopped and went into the church to pray. This regular praying together was a strong bond between them and their God. Though Chad was away much, he prayed at the same time as his brethren and so felt he was still at one with them.

Trumbert, a student of Chad's and later to become a teacher of the Venerable Bede, noticed on more than one occasion that there was another sound that caused Chad to stop what he was doing and turn to prayer; it was the sound of a storm. Whatever Chad was involved in, whether it was reading, writing or talking to someone, if the wind was strong he stopped and prayed then and there. Often he would say to a visitor, 'Come pray with me for all travellers, all who are upon the sea, and all whose lives are in danger. Let us remember all who forget God and His power.' If the wind rose to storm force he would close his book and kneel low before the Lord, devoting himself to more prayer. If the rain grew in strength and there was thunder and lightning, Chad would leave whatever he was doing and go into the church. In the church Chad would prostrate himself before the altar and pray to the Lord. He would stay there many a long hour, reciting psalms and uttering prayers until the storm passed over. When Trumbert asked him about this, Chad replied, 'I remember terrible winds and storms on Lindisfarne. I remember ships wrecked at sea. It is the storms that remind me how frail we are and how powerful is our God.' Chad continued, 'Have you not heard it said, "The Lord also thundered in the heavens and the Highest gave out His voice. Yes, He has sent His arrows out and scattered them: He shot forth His lightning and discomforted them." Trumbert, know that it is the Lord Himself who moves the air and raises the winds, the Lord hurls the lightning flash and thunders from heaven. He seeks to rouse the people out of their sleep, that they would see His power and turn to Him. He seeks them to come to him in awe, and to remember that there is a day when the earth will burn like fire and we will all be judged. He reminds us of the day when He will scatter the proud in their conceit, when He will come on the clouds in great power. He will come to judge the living and the dead. Pray that we will be found ready and awake at His coming. For this reason I take heed of God's display of power and respond to His heavenly warning with love and fear. As often as the sky is riven and God spares us, we should give thanks to Him for His love and mercy. We should give thanks for His grace and goodness towards us. We should examine our innermost being, searching out the secrets of our hearts and purging ourselves of sin. Above all, let us behave in such a way that we do not deserve to be struck down, by adoring Him and doing His will. May the Lord find us ready for His coming. Amen.'

After two and a half years of travelling and hard work as a bishop, Chad showed signs of weakness. The brothers noticed that for a few days Chad had not been his usual self. He had not shared in the prayers, apart from in the little oratory, and had done no manual work. Chad knew that he had caught the plague, and he prayed, 'Lord, if it be your will, spare me to continue your work. If it is your will that I depart from hence, let me come to you and share with you in your kingdom.' Seven of the brethren had gone off to the church and he was left alone in the oratory. Owini was working not far away in the vegetable patch. It was February and Chad felt a chill in his bones which he knew was more than the cold of winter. The chill of death was upon him.

Outside, Owini was breaking up the soil to let the frost get at it and kill off the weeds. He was bending over his spade when suddenly he heard the most beautiful singing, such as he had never heard before. At first he thought there must be a choir nearby and that the sound was travelling on the clear air. Then he thought it came from the oratory. Owini rested on his spade and listened. The song came from the sky. It was coming from the south-east, from the highest point of the winter sun. He could see nothing, but the sound was crystal clear; it seemed there was a procession of the heavenly hosts. As he was all attention the sound descended to the oratory, until it was over the roof where Chad was. 'I have no doubt that the sound was then heard from inside the building.

The beautiful sound filled the whole of the oratory and the whole of the surrounding area. I have never heard anything so beautiful in all my life and I do not believe I will hear the same again. I stood rapt in awe for what must have been about half an hour. I was not aware of the cold but rather of a strange warmth. I quietly joined my song with theirs and gave thanks for this wonder that was happening before me. I then became aware of the movement of the sound. I still did not see anything. The sound left the building and ascended, returning the way it came. I strained my ears and listened to what was an almost unbearable sweetness and beauty until it faded away.

'For a long time I did not move, I did not know what to do next. I strained my ears and my eyes but nothing was seen, only a robin, and it sang a few notes to the coming of spring. I was wondering what it all meant when suddenly the window of the oratory was thrown open and Chad started to loudly clap his hands together. Believe me, it made me jump. Mind you, this is the way Chad often attracted our attention. If he wanted any of us to come to him in the oratory he would clap his hands as loud as he could. I hurried over to see what he wanted. In the oratory I noticed that Chad's face seemed radiant with joy. "Owini, go quickly and bring the brothers from the church. Ask the seven of them to come here into the oratory and you come with them. I have some important things to tell you all."

'I wanted to stay and ask about what I had heard, but he hurried me out. I could tell by the excitement in his voice that this was important. The brothers were surprised to be recalled so quickly and asked me what it was about. At this stage I said nothing and told them I did not know.

'When we all came together, Chad sounded very serious. He said he was concerned that we kept the Rule that he had given to us. I am sure he was not worried about us taking on the Rule of Benedict, he wanted us to live fully by the Rule that he had taught. He told us that the Rule was for the well-being of the community. He had learnt most of the Rule from Aidan, and added to it from Rathmelsigi and from what he had read of the Fathers of the Church. For a while he talked of Cassian and the Desert Fathers. He asked us to live godly and virtuous lives. "Live in love and peace with each other and with all the faithful. Remember, there is no room for divisions and quarrels in the Church. If we are not at one with each other we cannot be at one with God. Pray for peace, live in peace, and share your peace with all. The peace of God be always with you."

'Suddenly, with his face glowing, Chad said, "Brothers, the day of my departure is at hand. I shall soon be taken away from you, for that beloved visitor who has been visiting many of our brethren has come for me also. Cedd has visited me this day and called me to join him in a new venture. He calls me away from this world into the kingdom of light. I do not want you to weep or mourn, but to rejoice, for I am to enter the fullness of life which is eternal. I know this to be true, for this day I have been told it is so."'

No one dared to speak, though Owini noticed there were tears in the eyes of nearly everyone. For a while they stood in silence, not knowing what to say or do. They could not imagine this little oratory, or the monastery, without their father Chad. With new energy Chad spoke again: 'Go now, return to the church and tell the rest of the brethren what I have told you. Ask them to pray for me and to commend my soul to Almighty God. Remember, we are all but mortal and need the grace and goodness of God. Prepare for your own departure, for it will come one day. Prepare with fasting, prayer and with a godly life. Let the Lord find you ready when He comes.' Chad started to cough and the strain of the coughing told on his weak body. He held up his hands for silence and asked them all to bow their heads so that he could send them away with his blessing.

> God, the creator of all things, keep you in
>   his love.
> Christ the Redeemer, keep you in his peace.
> The Holy Spirit of God sanctify and guide you.
> The Holy Three be ever about you.
> And the blessing of God Almighty, the Father,
>   the Son and the Holy Spirit, be among
>   you all, now and for evermore.

The brothers knew that they had been dismissed; silence descended and they all filed out without saying a word.

When they had all gone, Owini returned to the oratory where Chad was praying in silence. Aware that someone had entered, Chad after a while looked up to see Owini at the door. 'Come in, dear friend, and tell me what it is that is troubling you.' Owini hardly dared look at Chad. With his eyes downcast, Owini said, 'Father, I pray that you will let me ask you a question.' Chad said nothing but nodded his head. Owini also said nothing, not knowing where to start. Chad smiled and took Owini's gnarled hand into his. 'Ask what you will,' said Chad, knowing what was to come. Then Owini said, 'Father, I was working outside, digging over some of the land when I heard joyful voices in the air; the sound seemed to come from heaven itself. I am certain that these voices – I cannot call them any other as I saw nothing – came down to where you are here in the oratory. The place of prayer seemed full of music and beautiful sound for a long time and then the voices returned to the heavenly place and faded from my hearing. I want to know what it all means.'

Chad for a moment put his fingers to his lips and then smiling said, 'My dearest friend, you have been allowed to hear what no one else has heard. I command you in the name of the Lord to tell no one of this matter yet. I do not want anyone to know of this until after my death. If we are not careful, people will be attracted for the wrong reasons. You do understand, don't you?' Owini nodded. Chad continued, 'Today, in this place, I have been visited by angels who came to take me with them into the kingdom of heaven. I long to be there, though I will find parting difficult. I asked the angels that I may have a little time to put things in order. The heavenly host have promised to return, and in seven days will take me with them. Time is short, my friend, and there is much we need to do. Each day I will make arrangements and see to various people. I pray that you will all live in peace and keep the Rule.'

Owini turned away to hide a tear; he promised that he would tell no one. From that day onwards Chad became weaker in body though strangely

116

rested in mind and spirit. He was like someone resting before a special event. Each day he talked to his brethren as long as he was physically able, and spent much time in the oratory. He could be heard intoning litanies of his own.

Have mercy on me, O Lord,
bear me up on eagle's wings.
Have mercy on me, O Lord,
give your angels charge over me.
Have mercy on me, O Lord,
deliver me from the shadow of death.
Have mercy on me, O Lord,
call me into your glorious light.
Have mercy on me, O Lord,
bring me to the brightness of your presence.
Have mercy on me, O Lord,
lift me to the life that knows no end.

Owini looked after him and saw to any of his needs. On the seventh day, 2nd March, 672, Chad received the blessed sacrament of our Lord. He prayed, 'Now let your servant depart in peace according to your word; for my eyes have seen your salvation.' For a little while he rested. He seemed excited: 'Soon I shall see and know and love. O Lord, make me to be numbered with your saints in that glory which is everlasting.' It was with such joyful expectation that he died and entered into the glory of the kingdom of heaven.

A good while after Chad's death an abbot called Highbald from the province of Lindsey visited Chad's old friend Egbert. They talked about holy men and women, and of people who had influenced their lives for the good. Both of them spoke with fondness of Chad. Egbert said, 'I know a man on this island, who is still alive, and who saw a vision at the time of Chad's death. He saw the soul of Cedd descend from the heavens with a host of angels and then return to the heavenly kingdom, taking Chad's soul with him.' So the love of the brothers continued, for that which we build in this world is that which we take into the next.

Of Chad's brethren, Trumbert became the teacher of Bede and so told him much about Lastingham, Mercia and Chad. Winifrith, another of Chad's students, a good and discreet man, who was Chad's deacon for a long time, became the next Bishop of Lichfield. It seems that Owini may have gone to Ely to the monastery of his dear Etheldreda. Chad, like a candle, had burnt himself out, bringing light and warmth and hope to others.

EXERCISES

The soul of Chad's brother Cedd descended from the sky with a host of angels and returned to the heavenly kingdom, taking Chad's soul with him (Bede, Book 4, Chapter 3, 1992).

1   Read Psalm 34 verses 1–9.

I will bless the Lord at all times;
his praise shall ever be in my mouth.

I will glory in the Lord;
let the humble hear and rejoice.

Proclaim with me the greatness of the Lord;
let us exalt his name together.

I sought the Lord and he answered me
and delivered me out of all my terror.

Look upon him and be radiant,
and let not your faces be ashamed.

I called in my affliction and the Lord heard me
and saved me from all my troubles.

The angel of the Lord encompasses those who
   fear him,
and he will deliver them.

Taste and see that the Lord is good;
happy are they who trust in him!

Fear the Lord, you that are his saints,
for those who fear him lack nothing.

2   *Give thanks for the life of Chad. Pray for the
    diocese of Lichfield*

O holy Chad, be our advocate with the Lord, that
he may rule and guide us to heavenly mansions,
where with you and the saints we may for ever
dwell.

('Sarum Breviary')

3 *Pray.*

God be in my head, and in my understanding;
God be in my eyes, and in my looking;
God be in my mouth, and in my speaking;
God be in my heart, and in my thinking;
God be at mine end and in my departing.

(Source unknown)

Recommended Reading

R. Hyett Warner, *Life and Legends of St Chad*, Leach and Sons, Wisbech, 1871.

C. E. Whiting, *St Chad*, St Chad's College, 1986.

Jennie Austerberry, *Chad, Bishop and Saint*. English Life Publications, 1984.

Daibhi O Croinin, *Early Medieval Ireland*, Longman, 1995.

Lisa M. Bitel, *Isle of the Saints*, Cornell University Press, 1990.

Marina Smyth, *Understanding the Universe in Seventh Century Ireland*, Boydell Press, 1996.

Judith McClure and Roger Collins, eds., *The Ecclesiastical History of the English People*, World Classics Edition, Oxford University Press, 1994.

Acknowledgements and Sources

The Psalms are taken from the *Standard Book of Common Prayer* of the Episcopal Church of the USA, with the adaptations (including British English and inclusive language) as in *Celebrating Common Prayer* (Mowbrays 1992).

Bible readings are from the *New International Version*, copyright © 1973, 1978, 1984 by the International Bible Society. Published by Hodder & Stoughton.

The prayers with no acknowledgement are the author's own compositions.

The Bede extracts beginning the exercise sections are from *Bede's Ecclesiastical History of the English People*, edited by Bertram Colgrave and R. A. B. Mynors, Oxford University Press, 1992.

Sources of other prayers and hymns are as follows:

'All shall be Amen and Alleluia...' (page 76), St Augustine of Hippo, quoted in *An African Prayer Book*, p. 6, Desmond Tutu, Hodder & Stoughton, 1995.

'Blessed Lord, who has caused...' (page 36), *The Book of Common Prayer of 1662*, the rights in which are vested in the Crown's patentee, reproduced by permission of Cambridge University Press.

'Bless to me, O God...' (page 98), from *Carmina*

Gadelica, Vol. 3, p. 181, Alexander Carmichael, Scottish Academic Press, 1976.

'May I be no man's enemy...' (page 88), Eusebius, quoted in *A Time to Pray*, p. 58, compiled by Philip Law, Lion, 1997.

'O holy Chad...' (page 119), from the 'Sarum Breviary', *Life and Legends of St Chad*, R. Hyett Warner, Leach & Sons, 1891.

Rule of Comgall (page 45), the author's adaptation, from *The Celtic Monk: Rules and Writings of Early Irish Monks*, translated by Uinseann O'Maidin OCR, Cistercian Publications Inc, 1996.

'To elude nature...' (page 98), from *Practical Mysticism*, p. 90, Evelyn Underhill, E. P. Dutton and Co, 1943.